Your Towns and Cities in ... ...

York
in the Great War

For

Jac
Mum & Dad

Your Towns and Cities in the Great War

York
in the Great War

Karyn Burnham

Pen & Sword
MILITARY

First published in Great Britain in 2014 by
PEN & SWORD MILITARY
an imprint of
Pen and Sword Books Ltd
47 Church Street
Barnsley
South Yorkshire S70 2AS

ISBN 978 1 78337 609 4

A CIP record for this book is available from the British Library

Printed and bound in England
by Page Bros., Norwich

Typeset in Times New Roman by Chic Graphics

Pen & Sword Books Ltd incorporates the imprints of
Pen & Sword Archaeology, Atlas, Aviation, Battleground, Discovery,
Family History, History, Maritime, Military, Naval, Politics, Railways,
Select, Social History, Transport, True Crime, and Claymore Press,
Frontline Books, Leo Cooper, Praetorian Press, Remember When,
Seaforth Publishing and Wharncliffe.

For a complete list of Pen and Sword titles please contact
Pen and Sword Books Limited
47 Church Street, Barnsley, South Yorkshire, S70 2AS, England
E-mail: enquiries@pen-and-sword. co. uk
Website: www. pen-and-sword. co. uk

Contents

Acknowledgements

There are several people who contributed to this work in many ways, both large and small. My grateful thanks first to Hugh and Gill Murray, for allowing me to rifle through their extensive collection of photographs and postcards of York; this book would have been bereft of images without them. Thanks also to Sarah Sheils, historian and archivist for The Mount School, for allowing access to the *Mount School Magazine* and for many useful snippets of information; similarly to Jenny Orwin, archivist at Bootham School, for loaning me a corner of her office and access to the *Bootham School Magazine* and archives. Thanks to York Castle Museum for helping me get started and to Sarah Rees-Jones at IPUP, University of York, for permission to use images; particular thanks to James Maxton of Nestlé for his help with Rowntree's images; and the staff of the Borthwick Institute for Archives at the University of York.

Thanks is also due to Roni Wilkinson at Pen & Sword Ltd for his patience and understanding during a difficult time and to Jen Newby for her ceaseless support, advice and common sense. Thanks, finally, to Pam, as always.

Preface

The Founding of a City

The City of York has been shaped by every period in history, its identity continuing to evolve over almost 2,000 years of habitation. In AD 71, 5,000 soldiers of the Ninth Legion of the Roman Army founded the fortress town of Eboracum at the point where the River Foss joins the River Ouse. It was an ideal location for Romans, providing a sound base from which to launch attacks on the north of England and was easy to defend, due to the natural boundaries provided by the rivers. Within a few generations, the strategic importance of Eboracum was established and it began to grow into a thriving city, home briefly to two Roman emperors.

Long after the Romans had left York, the Anglo Saxons made the city their own, dismantling many of the Roman buildings and using the stone for other purposes. Eboracum evolved into Eoforwic and became an important trading port. York Minster, the city's most famous landmark, has its origins during the Anglo Saxon period, when a small wooden church was built on the spot where the minster is today.

While the Anglo Saxon leaders were occupied with celebrating the festival of All Saints Day on 1 November 866, Viking raiders attacked and the city evolved once more. Jorvik, as the city was now known, became the jewel in the Viking Kingdom of Northumbria. Viking rule lasted almost a hundred years, ending around AD 954. The Vikings' legacy in York remained and the city enjoyed continuing economic success; by AD 1000, York's population was second only to London.

When England was irrevocably united after the Norman invasion of 1066, William I was determined to bring the prosperous city of York into line and stamp out any notions of rebellion in the north. William ousted northern noblemen of Danish descent and replaced them with his own men; he built two castles in the city, one on either side of the

River Ouse, between which a chain could be drawn across the river to hamper access by boat. York was the only city outside London to have two castles, once again emphasising its importance.

Over the next five centuries, York developed into a layout that citizens and visitors would still recognise today. The walls were repaired and rebuilt until they encircled the city, with entrance gained through one of four 'bars' or gateways – Bootham Bar, Micklegate Bar, Walmgate Bar and Monk Bar – still impressive more than 500 years later. York Castle was built around 1244 as a base for Henry III, in preparation for war with Scotland; its keep was constructed at the top of a mound, known today as Clifford's Tower. The spectacular minster had a somewhat chequered path through the Norman and early Mediaeval period, being badly damaged by fire, then attacked by both the Danes and the Normans during various conflicts and claims on the city. In 1220, work began on the structure that still stands today, with the cathedral finally consecrated in 1472; York Minster remains the second largest Gothic cathedral in Northern Europe.

An intricate network of narrow streets and 'ginnels' developed – half-timbered, uneven shops and houses hunkered down in the shadow of the newly completed minster – the most famous of which, The Shambles, remains largely unaltered.

At the beginning of the twentieth century, York was a modern, thriving city, due largely to the railway which came to the city in 1839. In 1840, a direct line to London was opened and by the 1850s, thirteen trains a day were running between York and London. In 1877 a new station was opened, the largest in the country at that point – and by 1888, nearly 300 trains were arriving in York every day. A letter posted in London before noon could be delivered in York that same evening – a feat we can barely manage in the twenty-first century.

Thanks to the railway, York's economy boomed; industry went from strength to strength as manufacturers could easily trade anywhere in the country and tourists flocked to the city from far and wide. What they came to see was the very thing that made York unique: the long and varied history built into the fabric of the city. York residents often took this for granted, yet it still had the capacity to inspire and enthral.

On the face of it, the four years that represent the duration of the First World War may seem an insignificant drop in the ocean of York's long and tumultuous history. As I began my research for *York in the*

Great War, however, it soon became obvious that were I to attempt to record all aspects of life in York during the period 1914 -1918, then I would have to write a much bigger book and possibly more than one volume. I decided instead to research specific areas of life in York and above all, to look at human stories of people at their best and at their worst, living through an unimaginable war and coping with all the changes then being wrought upon their lives.

CHAPTER 1

The Unexpected War

At the beginning of 1914, life for the people of York went on in much the same way as it always had. The *Yorkshire Herald* reported sudden and uncharacteristic gale force winds in early March, causing 'Incidents In York Streets'. People went about the city on their daily business in a terribly British way, as schoolchildren were blown off their feet while crossing the road and adults were spotted clinging on to railings to avoid being carried off by the 'hurricane force' winds howling down the narrow streets. Some brave, but foolhardy souls attempted to get about by bicycle and, as in the case of at least one lady, were blown from their cycles and sent skittering down the road, machine and all.

Postcard entitled A Breezy Day in Old York – Courtesy of Hugh Murray.

York Tram on Davygate – Courtesy of Hugh Murray.

Elsewhere, repairs were being carried out on Monk Bar, one of the ancient entrances to the city, stoic through centuries of change. The repairs captured the public imagination because they involved the lowering of the portcullis, an event not seen for over a generation. Whereas once the portcullis would have been lowered to keep the city safe from invasion, now it prompted and welcomed an invasion of

Aerial view of River Foss and River Ouse – Courtesy of Hugh Murray.

Aerial view of York – Courtesy of Hugh Murray.

sightseers. According to the *Yorkshire Herald*, thousands arrived throughout the day to witness the spectacle. Citizens thronged alongside visitors from surrounding towns, villages and further afield. The *Herald* reported that 'as many as fifty photographs were taken'.

York had long been a proud garrison town. Cavalry barracks were established in the Fulford area in 1795, as part of William Pitt's barrack building scheme with the Ancient British Fencibles being the first regiment to occupy the site. Over the next eighty years or so, the barracks continued to develop, with a new military hospital built in 1854 on the other side of the Fulford Road accommodating 120 patients, followed by the construction of a church in 1867 and a military prison in 1884; by 1900, York Castle was also being used as a military prison.

The *Yorkshire Gazette* records that there were twenty four officers and 707 other ranks in residence at Fulford barracks by 1909. The Headquarters of the North-Eastern Military District moved from Manchester to York in 1878, with York becoming the Headquarters of Northern Command in 1905. The War Office purchased 1,800 acres of Strensall Common to the south of the city and established Strensall Camp in 1884; six years later, workshops and a wharf were constructed for the Royal Army Ordnance Corps.

York residents were accustomed to a local military presence, which waxed and waned according to the wider political situation. For the first seven months of 1914, there was nothing unusual in the presence of soldiers in York; there was no massing of troops or indication that a conflict was just around the corner. Neither were the authorities unduly concerned about the size of their territorial forces; the *Yorkshire Herald* reported in early May 1914 a territorial force of 14,433 men and 543 officers – an increase of 1,248 men since December 1913. A recruitment drive also featured in the *Herald*, with a statement by Lieutenant C.C. Pickles of 5th Battalion Yorkshire Regiment: 'A few smart recruits are still required. . . who will receive 15s on attestation and any person bringing them will receive 5s.' Little did anyone know just how insignificant those numbers would seem in a few short months.

In May 1914, the city decked out its streets to celebrate Military Sunday, a York tradition established in 1885 when Dean Purey-Cust had organised a service and parade to commemorate the death of General Gordon of Khartoum. Despite the morning of Sunday 11 May

Military Sunday before World War I – Courtesy of Hugh Murray.

being unseasonably cold, crowds gathered outside the minster from 8.30 am; some queuing patiently, others jostling for a better position, each in possession of a brown, blue or red ticket which guaranteed them a place inside for the service. As the morning progressed, the streets around the minster, the city centre and beyond began to fill up with onlookers all hoping to secure the best place from which to view the parade following the service.

Every section of the armed services were represented on Military Sunday, including cavalry, artillery and infantry: 1,800 troops in total. When the service in the minster was over, the troops took to the streets from noon and York was treated to a 'striking military spectacular', which attracted visitors from far and wide and invoked 'stirring street scenes'. The military parade was followed immediately by an equally impressive civic procession, led by the great and good of York.

Olive Burton was about to celebrate her fourteenth birthday when she witnessed the spectacle of what was to be the last Military Sunday before the outbreak of war. Olive's family lived close to the city's Fulford Road barracks, so soldiers and cavalry were a familiar sight for her, but Military Sunday was an excitement not to be missed. In an unpublished memoir, Olive recalled being dazzled by the full colour and splendour of the military uniforms, the scarlet tunics set off by gold braid and brass, the sheen of the expertly groomed horses and marching bands playing tunes which swelled the heart with patriotic pride.

For York, as for every other town and city throughout Britain, the first half of 1914 was no different to the years preceding it. No one could have foreseen the cataclysmic consequences of the assassination of a foreign Archduke in a distant land. The causes of the First World War are well documented and have been analysed many times elsewhere, so they do not bear repeating in detail here. With the benefit of hindsight though, we can look back on a clear timeline of events that led to the assassination of Archduke Ferdinand on 28 June 1914. We can then chart the subsequent political fallout that saw Austria-Hungary garnering support from her more powerful ally, Germany, while Serbia secured the backing of Russia. Ultimatums were issued and brinksmanship pushed to the limit until finally, on 3 August, Germany declared war on France and mobilised her troops to attack France's more sparsely defended borders with Belgium.

Up to this point, Britain had been watching the escalating

aggression from the sidelines; the government saw the issue as a European problem, not something with which Britain should become involved. Even as late as 1 August, the government had reassured the British people that it had no intention of becoming caught up in a European war. When Germany made the decision to invade Belgium to get at France, however, Britain's attitude to the conflict changed overnight. Belgium was a neutral country and the ports of Ostend and Zeebrugge were vital for Britain's continental trade. Belgium's neutrality was protected by the 1839 Treaty of London, which stated that the 'guarantor countries (of which Britain was one) had the right to intervene in order to defend the neutrality of Belgium'. On 3 August, the British Foreign Secretary, Sir Edward Grey, sent an ultimatum to Germany to withdraw its troops from Belgium by 11pm the following day or face a declaration of war from Britain.

The Early Days of War

In response to Grey's ultimatum, excitement swept the country and crowds gathered on the streets of London. The *Daily Mirror* reported that the King, Queen, Prince of Wales and Princess Mary had appeared on the balcony of Buckingham Palace at 8pm to the 'wild, enthusiastic cheers' of a 'record crowd'. As the 11pm deadline for Germany's response approached, the crowds grew quiet, waiting for the chimes of Big Ben before erupting into cheering and shouting which, according to *The Times*, 'echoed. . . for nearly twenty minutes' before the King re-appeared on the balcony and the crowd began to sing the National Anthem.

Scenes like this were repeated throughout the country; factories sounded their sirens to inform workers that the country was at war and word was communicated to feverish gatherings in public places. In York, the news was announced on the morning of 5 August to crowds gathered outside the offices of the *Yorkshire Herald* newspaper on Coney Street and, as in London, was greeted with loud and prolonged cheering and spontaneous singing of the National Anthem.

The actual declaration of war came as a surprise to many Britons and was met with a mix of anxiety and excitement. Two days later, on 7 August, the *York Press* ran a feature entitled 'HOW TO BE USEFUL', which offered advice to citizens of York on how to react to the news of war and how to conduct themselves in this time of crisis:

• First and foremost – keep your heads. Be calm. Go about your ordinary business quietly and soberly. Do not indulge in excitement or foolish demonstration.

• Secondly – Think of others more than you are wont to do. Think of your duty to your neighbour. Think of the common weal.

• Try to contribute your share by doing your duty in your own place and your own sphere.

• Do not store goods and create an artificial scarcity to the hurt of others. Remember that it is an act of mean and selfish cowardice.

• Do what you can to cheer and encourage our soldiers. Gladly help any organisation for their comfort and welfare.

• Explain to the young and ignorant what war is and why we have been forced to wage it.

This generally sound, sensible advice amounted to a call to 'keep calm and carry on'. It is unclear how much of this advice was speculative and how much was formed in response to the actual behaviour of residents, but another article, also published in the *York Press* that same day, gives us some insight into the 'mean and selfish cowardice' mentioned above.

PUBLIC MUST STOP PANIC RUSH

There has again been a mad rush on the part of the public to secure reserve stocks of what can only be called panic prices.

The article then lists the rapid increase of prices in York of butter, York ham, Wiltshire bacon and cheeses, before reporting that:

In view of the Government assurances as to the supply of wheat, the millers have today reduced the price of flour from 40s-45s a sack to 35s. The retailers have in consequence reduced the price. It is hoped that the general public will not abuse this move and thus force the retailers to raise the price against the poor who cannot afford to buy in at one time more than the normal week's supply.

This plea for calm to stabilise prices did not seem to have any long term effect. In January 1915, G. Dickinson, secretary of the York Grocers' Association, produced figures showing that flour had gone up from 25s 6d at the beginning of 1914 to 42s twelve months later. A correspondent for the *Herald* claimed that prices were higher in York than in other areas of the country, citing pineapples as an example: they were apparently selling in London for 10d, but cost a princely 3s 6d in York.

Inevitably, because of its central location, York soon began to fill with soldiers as troops arrived in the city on their way to the south coast and departure for Belgium or France. The *York Press* reported that troops were arriving by train in York 'hourly' and were being dealt with at the station in 'a prompt and businesslike manner'. The *Press* also describes the heavily loaded troop trains which passed through York without stopping; poignantly, the platforms were 'showered with letters' flung from the train windows by departing soldiers. Any letters that missed the platforms and landed on the rails were quickly collected by 'agile porters and keen passengers waiting for trains.' Many of the letters had been hastily penned and the envelopes lacked stamps, but they were collected up and posted anyway.

Across the city, the functions of public buildings began to change in response to the demands of war. The former Exhibition Buildings, now York Art Gallery, were requisitioned as a military headquarters and recruitment centre for the duration of the war, while the Central Hall was transformed into the city's post office. This post office soon became a lifeline to thousands, as it organised the letters and parcels sent overseas to loved ones and ensured that the longed-for letters from soldiers at the Front made it home. All the letters collected from those passing trains were brought here and processed for delivery, whether franked or not.

As the city began to fill up with troops, providing temporary billets for them became a priority and this often meant the requisition of public spaces, like the racecourse on the Knavesmire and several of York's schools. The *York Press* posted a notice to parents, informing them that seven public elementary schools in the city would not re-open for the autumn term on 10 August, 'as the buildings have been requisitioned for the accommodation of troops'.

Sure enough, on the night of 6 August, 300 men of the 5th West

The Main Hall of York's Exhibition Buildings (now York Art Gallery) being used as the city's main post office during the Great War – With permission of IPUP.

Exterior of the Exhibition Buildings – With permission of IPUP.

YMCA Camp in York – courtesy of Hugh Murray.

Yorkshire regiment arrived from Harrogate to find themselves sleeping on make-shift beds on the floor of the assembly hall of Haxby Road School. The 2nd Dragoon Guards' Reserve fared a little better; when they arrived in York all the way from Dunbar, they were billeted at the Fulford Road barracks to wait for their horses to arrive before travelling on. By the end of September, around 2,400 men were billeted at the cavalry barracks and the racecourse was provided with 1,500 beds to accommodate the 5th Cavalry Reserve.

Young Olive Burton, who lived close to the barracks, remembered the increased activity, the constant coming and going at all hours of day and night and the apparent 'change' in troops entering and leaving the barracks. Rather than gleaming in highly polished brass, horses and riders were now dull and drab; Olive also wondered whether some of the horses had been dyed black, as there no longer seemed to be any with pale hair.

As York began to burst at the seams with figures in khaki, the *York Press* noted with surprise that Strensall Camp remained empty, with

Cavalry crossing Skeldergate Bridge – Courtesy of Hugh Murray.

Fulford Barracks – Courtesy of Hugh Murray.

'no influx of troops expected'. Strensall Camp had seemed the ideal place for troops to be based, because they could be quickly despatched to the east coast in the event of an invasion, while 'in the meantime affording them unique opportunities of improving their marksmanship'. By the end of October, however, the camp was occupied by as many as 7,000 troops.

This rapid swelling of York's population led to some remarkable acts of philanthropy as the community were determined to play some small part in the war effort. Appeals were made for mundane items such as blankets and crockery for the billeted soldiers, along with collections for cigarettes and even saddles and binoculars. Very soon, knitting circles began to spring up, producing scarves, socks, balaclavas and anything else that could be usefully created with a pair of needles and some wool. Olive Burton's mother played her part by making up to twenty shirts (or 'greybacks' as they were known) per week and Olive was given the task of putting five button-holes in each shirt.

Some schools in York were requisitioned, not as temporary billets but as auxiliary hospitals in anticipation of a potential naval attack on the east coast causing dozens, if not hundreds, of casualties. In an unpublished memoir of her time in York during the war, Agnes Smithson, the daughter of a textile manufacturer in Halifax, recorded that she was to join the Mount School, a Quaker school for girls, in August 1914; but it, along with Bootham School, was requisitioned as a hospital. Both schools were kitted out with a hundred beds and nursing staff, but their conversion to hospitals only lasted a matter of weeks until it became obvious that the fighting was going to happen in mainland Europe and no large scale naval attack on Britain was imminent. The Mount School was hastily turned back into an educational establishment and Agnes began her school career only a little later than planned.

A Call to Arms

The British Army, even when fully mobilised, was comparatively small in 1914 – just one sixth the size of the German Army, so a massive injection of recruits was needed, and quickly. The surge of patriotic fervour, the popular belief that it 'would all be over by Christmas' and, perhaps, a boyish desire for adventure, prompted men to flock in their thousands to recruiting stations across Britain. In the first week of the

5th Battalion Yorks and Lancs Regiment ready for inspection, spring 1915 – Courtesy of Hugh Murray.

Inspection of York YT Corps – Courtesy of Hugh Murray.

war, 8,193 men joined up, then 43,354 in the second, 63,000 in the third and an incredible 174,901 in the fourth week alone. Before the war was one month old, almost 300,000 men had volunteered to fight for King and country. Secretary of State for War, Lord Kitchener, believed however, that the war would stretch far beyond Christmas and probably continue for at least three years. Consequently, in the early weeks of September, he launched a national recruitment campaign.

York, like every other town and city in the country, played its part in the call to arms. From the opening days of the war, the local papers featured daily notices politely recalling old soldiers to their regiments. The papers in those early days were a jumble of mixed messages representative of a country not yet used to the implications of being at war. Alongside a notice advertising the Great Bank Holiday Attractions at the Empire Theatre, York, for example, was the following:

MOBILIZATION

ALL EX-TERRITORIAL SOLDIERS WHO ARE WILLING
TO REJOIN THE COLOURS
SHOULD REPORT THEMSELVES EITHER PERSONALLY
OR IN WRITING
TO THEIR FORMER CORPS WITHOUT DELAY
HORATIO MENDS
Brigadier General,
Secretary.

After the initial rush to enlist, the number of men willing to join up gradually tapered off, not just in York but across the whole country. One particular barrier to recruitment in York, it seems, was not the fear of going to war *per se*, but tied up with far more domestic concerns. An ordinary soldier's pay was lower than that of a skilled labourer, for example, so for those men who had secure jobs and families to support, their joining the army would mean hardship for their wives and children. Not only that, but they also feared what might happen to their jobs while they were away; there was no guarantee of being taken back on in the same position or with the same pay.

In response to this issue, some York employers took the radical step of offering financial support for employees wishing to enlist. Henry

Leetham's Flour Mill – Courtesy of Hugh Murray.

Leetham of Leetham Flour Mills undertook to 'make up' the wages of men joining up for the duration of the war. Rowntree's also promised to 'look after' the families of enlisted men until the end of 1914; their jobs would be kept open and pension premiums would be paid too. With hindsight, it is obvious that these generous offers were made in the belief that the war would indeed be over by Christmas.

There were some, of course, who took a less philanthropic view towards persuading men to enlist. In a furious letter to the *York Press*, a W. F. Wailes-Fairbairn of Askham Richard called for the ostracism and shaming of those men unwilling to fight, while another letter sent to the York Board of Guardians by the Sedgefield Union suggested that all 'vagrants' in the city between the ages of 18 and 30 be rounded up and 'in some way utilised'. This rather alarming suggestion was thrown out by the Board because it amounted to compulsory service which, if that was to be the case, should be compulsory for all, not just those unlucky enough to be considered 'vagrants'.

The entertainment industry in York was also determined to play its part in the recruitment drive; at the end of August, a 'patriotic night' was organised at the Theatre Royal by the manager, Mr E.W. Silverthorne, in order to encourage enlistment and raise money for charitable work in York. Mr Silverthorne invited the Boy Scouts in York, along with the nurses of York County Hospital and other institutions to attend a performance of *Charley's Aunt*. All were to wear full uniform.

Despite the best efforts of those concerned, recruitment in York still fell short of other towns and cities, though contemporary press reports create a somewhat contradictory picture. The *Yorkshire Herald* ran an optimistic piece, describing how the staff at the recruiting depot in the newly-requisitioned Exhibition Buildings were 'still busy at work' at midnight and it was believed that 'over 600 men have joined from the city of York since the Army Order was made and these include many old soldiers.' The piece finished with the declaration that 'all records at the York Depot were broken in one weekend.'

The *York Press* took a more measured approach with their piece. 'An average of 34 recruits per day,' it began, 'are being accepted at the York recruiting depot for Lord Kitchener's special army.' Although it agreed that these were 'excellent figures', the paper then argued that the city of York could 'take little credit for them as more than 93% of

(Above and below) Barbican cattle market, Walmgate, being used as a depot for war horses – With permission of IPUP.

the enlistments emanate from outside the [city] boundaries'. The piece finished by claiming that York is 'reputed to be one of the most difficult places in England for obtaining recruits'.

Not only men were being recruited from the streets of York in those early stages of the war. The army needed horses for the cavalry, but more importantly and in far greater numbers, for transport. Officers scoured the country, commandeering horses of every breed that appeared fit and of a reasonable age. A price would be offered, with little chance of negotiation or refusal, then a broad arrow was marked on the horse's hoof to indicate the sale. In York the animal would be taken off to the Barbican Road cattle market in the Walmgate area of the city, recently requisitioned by the military as a horse depot.

One old farmer from the outskirts of York had the ill-fortune to take his wife out for a drive on a day when the scouts were in the area. He was pulled up in the village of Stamford Bridge by the officers who, after examining the horse's mouth, offered him £40 for her. The farmer began to argue that this was his only horse and sole means of transport, therefore he had no intention of selling it, but his argument fell on deaf ears as the broad arrow was marked on the animal's hoof.

The role of 'war horses' during the First World War has been widely documented in recent years, many of the animals came from farms and were used to pulling ploughs and carts. Just like the men they served, they went into battle in the very worst of conditions and over half a million never came home again. When poisonous gas was introduced, gas masks were designed to protect horses as well as soldiers. One of these horse gas masks is on display at the Castle Museum in York.

Drunken Debauchery on the Streets of York

When thousands of soldiers are billeted together in the same city, inevitably they will spend the free time they have left enjoying themselves. In the first few months of the war, the publicans of York benefitted greatly and the young women of the city suddenly found themselves very popular. The moral implications of the situation soon began to cause concern and in September, the Lord Mayor of York and founder of Browns Department Store, Henry Rhodes Brown, pleaded with the city's young women 'to refrain from levity and from making difficulties for the recruits.' Even the Archbishop of York, Cosmo Gordon Lang, preached a sermon to the soldiers in which he asked them to refrain from drinking to excess and compromising ladies; citizens of York were also advised to curb their patriotic desire to buy the lads a drink. Lieutenant General Herbert Plumer, General Officer Commanding-in-Chief Northern Command, was so concerned by the effect of alcohol on his troops that he wrote to York's licensing magistrates, asking them to curb the opening hours of pubs.

As it happened, the Intoxicating Liquor (Temporary Restrictions) Act was passed at the end of August and this paved the way for pub opening hours to be restricted throughout the country. In September 1914, the pubs, clubs and eating houses of York were instructed to close between the hours of 9pm and 6am. The regulations prompted outrage, with letters in the *Herald* claiming curtailment of liberty and the city's publicans protesting loudly at the damage to their businesses, particularly in poorer areas of the city such as Walmgate, where pubs were numerous. To them, the restrictions in York seemed especially unfair when pubs in the West Yorkshire garrison town of Pontefract were allowed to stay open until 10pm and 10.30pm on Saturdays.

Concerns over excessive alcohol consumption continued to be raised throughout the war and many were aimed at women. With husbands away fighting, women received a separation allowance from the military and many also took a job to contribute to the war effort – for the first time, women had money of their own and a certain degree of independence. There were suggestions that some women were spending their separation allowance in the pub and that incidents of female drunkenness were on the increase.

In February 1915, an edition of the weekly Suffragette paper, *Votes for Women,* carried a report on an Army Council circular, which had allegedly called for wives of serving soldiers to be barred from public houses and for it to be made illegal to sell alcohol to them. In a speech made the following year, however, the new Lord Mayor of York, William Alexander Foster Todd, quoted statistics that seemed to utterly refute claims that the women of York were turning to drink. There were 1,200 soldiers' wives residing in York, he stated, but only twenty-five had committed offences related to drunkenness and seventeen of this number had already been 'familiar' to the authorities prior to the war.

No laws were passed barring women from public houses and, despite being banned from buying drinks for soldiers, fears of women 'chasing' after soldiers remained. The National Union of Women

Workers took up the mantle and proposed 'voluntary women's patrols' to seek out any suspected immoral behaviour by being 'true friends of the girls, in the deepest and holiest sense'. In York, the wives of local dignitaries founded a branch of the 'League of Honour for Women and Girls of the British Empire', which organised regular patrols around the streets, parks and cinemas of York. Volunteers ensured that women were behaving 'morally' and 'respectably'. Courting couples were chivied out of darkened doorways and dragged from under bushes while being lectured sternly on the error of their ways.

During the last few months of 1914, life in York had changed considerably. The deluge of khaki uniforms had increased the city's population, public buildings had taken on new roles, and regulations were introduced which restricted everyday life as never before. While many volunteered to fight for King and country or began fund raising and knitting supplies for the troops, some began hoarding food which forced prices up, denying a fair share to the less well off and others worried about women developing loose morals. As 1914 drew to a close, no-one knew just how long the war would last, nor how many lives it would take. The citizens of York had no idea that the walls of their ancient city would soon suffer a direct attack by the enemy.

CHAPTER 2

Aliens, Refugees and Zeppelins

The nation began to adapt to the swift changes in the fabric of British life during the last few months of 1914. The citizens of York accepted that factories, offices and mills were emptying of men, public buildings were being commandeered for official use and the rail network was filling up with men in khaki. A nationwide recruitment campaign began, with posters exploiting both national pride and personal shame as tools to persuade men to enlist. People became patriotic to an extent they never had been before, supporting the call to arms by encouraging their menfolk to join up and berating those who would not. Tolerance of those who were different also shifted as old prejudices resurfaced. From August 1914, anyone living in Britain who was German, of German descent or even had a faintly Germanic-sounding name, immediately fell under suspicion and York was no different in this.

Before the war, the government had compiled a register of 'non-naturalised' British residents to deal with what it termed the 'alien problem' and in the early days of the war the Alien Restrictions Act was passed by Parliament. This meant that the government now had powers to restrict the movements of aliens in Britain and further laws followed, prohibiting aliens from sending letters abroad, owning wireless sets, cameras, firearms, motor cars – the list goes on. Shortly after the Act became law, the government began to arrest non-naturalised German, Austrian and Hungarian males of military age, either repatriating or interning them. As the months went by, the government's powers widened and the authorities also began to close down premises either owned or frequented by aliens. Naturally, the suspicions of the establishment filtered down through society, until even the most innocent of German shopkeepers came to be seen as the enemy within. *The Daily Mail* demanded, 'Refuse to be served by a German Waiter', and Horatio Bottomley, editor of the *John Bull* magazine, made a vitriolic appeal:

> *I call for a vendetta against every German in Britain, whether 'naturalised' or not. You cannot naturalise an unnatural beast – a human abortion – a hellish freak. But you can exterminate it. And now the time has come. No German must be allowed to live in our land.*

Propaganda like this led to attacks on British citizens whose names happened to sound German and York was not immune to such prejudice in its attitudes to supposed aliens. One York resident, a Mr Joseph Foster Mandefield, was so appalled at the rumours circulating about him that he wrote to the *York Press* in an attempt to clarify his nationality. Mr Mandefield ran a hosiery business in Monkgate and shortly after the declaration of war he realised that some of his customers, knowing he was of European extraction, thought that his surname sounded Germanic. Mr Mandefield was, in fact, British and had lived in the same York parish all his life. He quickly scotched such notions by making it clear that his father's family had originated from France, *not* Germany, and continued about his business.

He had underestimated the strength of anti-German feeling in the city, however, and was horrified to discover that speculation about his heritage had developed into rumours, which in turn fermented into malicious slander. He was unfairly accused of being an enemy alien and stories were circulated that he had intended kill off half of York by poisoning the local reservoir, and that he had subsequently been arrested by the military and was languishing in prison. None of this had a scrap of credibility, but there was enough suspicion floating around to seriously damage both his business and his reputation. Mr Mandefield offered a £5 reward to anyone who could give information leading to the arrest of those responsible for circulating such damaging lies.

Mr Mandefield was not alone in being on the receiving end of spurious accusations. A Mr W. Kitching of Holgate also took to the *York Press* to defend his reputation, when it was widely suggested that he was the owner of a secret airship or aeroplane (the rumour-mongers could not decide which) and that he was using one of these contraptions to assist the enemy. Quite where Mr Kitching was supposed to be hiding his airship or aeroplane, or managing to use them, is unclear. Although these rumours annoyed Mr Kitching enough to prompt him to defend his name in print, he seemed more dismissive than outraged, stating simply: 'I have no desire to assist the enemy in any way whatever.'

In November 1914, the Archbishop of York, Cosmo Gordon Lang, spoke out against widespread anti-German propaganda, but his good intentions backfired when he accidentally caused offence by recalling the funeral of Queen Victoria, when Kaiser Wilhelm had knelt alongside his uncle, King Edward VII, before the coffin of the late Queen. The Archbishop had perhaps misjudged the national mood, as his remarks were branded pro-German and led to considerable public hostility towards Lang, which took several years to die down.

York's Concentration Camp

Although many of York's citizens were subjected to unfair speculation, thousands more were rounded up and arrested by the authorities. All non-naturalised British residents were arbitrarily arrested and imprisoned during the first few months of the war. In York, Mr Schumacher, a man in his sixties, was arrested while waiting for a tram in Acomb; he was considered 'dangerous' despite being married to an English woman and having a son serving in the Royal Garrison Artillery. Similarly, Julius Koch, a manager and long term employee at the Selby Olympia Mills, was arrested with several other employees; Herbert Lindenberg, an employee of the Ardol factory, and another eight men employed by the International Boring Company were also arrested simply for being German or of Germanic extraction.

These men were imprisoned in York Castle, which quickly filled up as more and more aliens were arrested and brought to York from far and wide. The prison accommodation spilled out on to Castle Green, where a tented encampment was erected to cope with the influx, but still more men came. The Exhibition Buildings, which operated as both

Tented internment camp on Castle Green – With permission of IPUP.

central Post Office and Recruiting Office, accepted a hundred men who were put up on straw mattresses. It became increasingly obvious that York could not accommodate the several hundred more prisoners who were expected over the following weeks and so an internment camp was hastily built along Leeman Road, on land once occupied by the York Engineering Company. By the end of September 1914, 13,600 enemy aliens were being held in internment camps in Britain, 10,500 of whom were civilians.

The camp on Leeman Road was consistently referred to as a 'concentration camp' by the contemporary press. Although for us this term conjures up horrific images of the Nazi persecution of Jews during the Second World War, back in 1914 it meant simply a camp where a concentration of a particular group of people were held. In the case of the Leeman Road camp, this group consisted of German and Austrian men – both aliens and prisoners of war.

Built just twenty-five yards away from the roadside, the Leeman Road concentration camp was a collection of wooden structures standing on concrete bases, complete with electric lighting. Separate buildings were allocated for sleeping accommodation, meals and luggage, with another structure fulfilling the role of hospital for up to twelve patients, although any inmate requiring specialist care was transferred to the Military Hospital on Fulford Road. There was a large exercise area but the whole site was enclosed by a 6ft high fence of barbed wire. Armed guards were posted around the perimeter fence, just in case any of the 1,600 inmates should try to make a run for it.

It is hard to imagine what impact this had on the lives of these men and their families, particularly for those who had been plucked from ordinary civilian lives. Surprisingly, coverage in the *York Press* implies that morale was high in the camp, with the men engaged in sporting pastimes and singing 'songs of the Fatherland'. By early October, almost all the prisoners had been moved from York Castle to the Leeman Road camp. Only three now remained in the Castle, one of whom, according to the *Herald*, spent a good deal of his time playing the concertina.

Many of the men interned in the Leeman Road camp had been unsure of where they would be sent after their arrest and therefore had brought luggage with them – often several cases each – so they were generally well prepared for their confinement. A shop in the camp sold cigarettes, while a barber's shop did a brisk trade under a sign that read 'Business as usual; all cash, no credit!' The men were kept busy with the day-to-day maintenance of the camp, performing the necessary duties on a rota basis.

The creation of the Leeman Road camp prompted a curious response, not only from the people of York, but from miles around. On Sunday afternoons, tourists and sightseers would flock to Leeman Road in their thousands to see the camp and its inmates. The phenomenon was reported in both the *York Press* and the *Herald*, with the *Herald* keen to emphasise that 'the numbers are not exaggerated.' The sightseers crowded around the perimeter of the camp, not to jeer or persecute the inmates as the general tide of anti-German feeling would suggest, but rather to converse with them, to cheer them up and even to throw 'apples and sweetmeats' over the fence for them. The *Herald* took a dim view of this behaviour and addressed its readership in a censorious tone. 'Who are these people who behave like yokels attending the Zoo?' it demanded, rebuking the crowds for their morbid curiosity in staring at the unhappy men, who included 'dangerous enemies to our land'.

The military authorities tried to warn people off visiting, even threatening to completely board up the perimeter fence of the camp. The *Herald* took the *Press* to task for publishing pictures of the camp, thereby exciting further public interest. The *Herald* was particularly concerned that the continuing spectacle would damage the reputation of York and suggested that all the able-bodied young men who visited on a Sunday should be in uniform and the women could better employ their time by knitting socks and making woollen shirts for those soldiers preparing for a hard winter at the Front.

Among the internees at the camp was August Burkert, a 39-year-old Austrian-born engineer, who had been detained because 'he was likely to become dangerous', despite having lived peaceably in Selby for many years. August went to the camp hospital building after becoming unwell; he reported that he had felt faint and clammy for several hours. The doctor checked him over, but apparently could find nothing wrong and so August was sent on his way. Several hours later, feeling much worse, August returned to the hospital building, where he collapsed. He had suffered a massive heart attack and, despite several attempts to revive him, died shortly after. A subsequent inquest found that, unbeknownst to August, he had been suffering from heart disease and, in the circumstances, his death could not have been prevented. He was buried in York and afforded a small funeral service, which several of his friends from the camp were allowed to attend.

The Leeman Road concentration camp was later closed down, due to overcrowding, and the internees were farmed out to various other similar camps around the country.

In the meantime, anti-German sentiment in York continued to grow, always worsening whenever there was particularly bad news of the war. When both nearby Scarborough and Hartlepool were shelled on 16 December 1914, resulting in eighty-two deaths and 250 casualties, Miss Edith Milner, a wealthy and influential York resident, wrote yet another of her many letters to the *Herald*. She argued that the attacks could only have happened with the help of 'the danger in our midst' and demanded to know why York did not have more stringent measures in place to restrict aliens.

The sinking of RMS *Lusitania* by a U-boat off the coast of Ireland on 7 May 1915, sparked an intense anti-German backlash across Britain. Attacks on businesses run by anyone with German connections grew and small scale riots broke out around the country. In the mining village of Goldthorpe, some forty miles south of York, twenty-three miners attacked a shop owned by a Fredrick Shonut; they burned his premises and broke into his house, causing around £1,300 worth of damage. A neighbour of Shonut and fellow shopkeeper, John Robert Bakewell, voiced his disapproval of the attack and in return had his own shop and home attacked by a mob, who made three attempts to burn his premises down. The debacle escalated into a full-blown riot with looting, baton charges and gunfire. In the process, Mr Bakewell, who had no German connections whatsoever, was hit on the head with a brick and had damage costing over £3,000 to repair done to his property.

Belgian Refugees

When Germany invaded Belgium at the beginning of August 1914, her troops moved through the country at speed and with force. The Belgian Army stubbornly resisted the invading forces wherever it could, rapidly turning some areas into war zones. Life in Belgium quickly became untenable for its people, as towns and villages were commandeered or ransacked and farms were burned. Belgians began to flee in their thousands, taking whatever belongings they could carry or cart with them. Column upon column of newly homeless and frightened Belgians flocked towards the country's borders, with almost 60,000 heading for Britain via Dunkirk and Calais.

The plight of the Belgians was well reported in the British press and there was great sympathy for the refugees as they began to arrive on British shores, because they brought home the reality of war. They embodied, after all, the cause that British soldiers were being sent to fight for. Even those who did not support the war in general terms saw the value of relief work. Within a day or two of war being declared, the National Relief Fund was launched and immediately began fund raising, with the aim of providing aid and relief for those affected by the war. As refugees began arriving, towns and cities throughout the country prepared to welcome and provide temporary homes for them.

The first contingent of Belgian refugees arrived in York on the evening of 6 October 1914. As they disembarked, dishevelled and exhausted, from the 5.40pm London train, they were met by ringing cheers from a station crowded with curious York residents ready to

Belgian Refugees in York – With permission of Sarah Shiels.

welcome the visitors to their city. The chairman of the relief committee, Mr E. Gray, and the Sheriff, Mr Newbald Kay, greeted them and led them to a fleet of cabs waiting to transport them to the Mansion House, where the Lady Mayoress and the local reception committee had organised refreshments.

This first group, like many others that followed, was a disparate assembly of the old, the young and families from all over Belgium. The children, some no more than eighteen months old, were wide-eyed and excited by the adventure, but the adults were weary, anxious and often traumatised by what they had witnessed. They had fled their homes some six weeks previously and had been travelling ever since. Many had horror stories to tell of fleeing from the German Army as their homes were invaded and attacked.

One man, a miner from a small village near Liége, told how he had run from his home with nothing more than the clothes on his back and three of his six children, while his wife had followed with the three younger children. He and the other residents had escaped the village on one road as German soldiers arrived along another. They had stopped to look back and had seen columns of smoke rising from their houses; the miner had noticed flames pouring out of his own cottage. In the chaos of flight, however, the miner had lost sight of his wife and three of his children and had not seen them since.

Another man, a citizen of Malines, described how he and his family had been sitting down to dinner one evening when a great outcry announced the arrival in the city of the German Army. There had been no time to finish their meal or pack up their belongings; the family left their house immediately and headed out of the city, along with thousands of others. He reported that those who were unfortunate enough to remain in the city had been killed by the invading troops.

The Quaker population of York had a particularly large part to play in the welcoming of Belgian refugees to the city. Pupils and staff of The Mount School, a Quaker school for girls, were involved in the organisation of meals, accommodation and entertainment for the refugees and also the subsequent billeting of families throughout the area. The Friends Meeting House in Friargate was hurriedly converted into temporary accommodation and accepted its first batch of refugees on 22 October. As before, the refugees arrived at the Meeting House in a convoy of cabs from the station and were greeted by crowds, who clapped and cheered them along the streets. The police ensured the road was clear outside the Meeting House and ceremoniously opened the door of each cab as it halted at the entrance. The tired travellers must have been bewildered by all the protocol and fuss after such a harrowing journey.

Their luggage, such as it was, accumulated in the Meeting House yard until it was piled high with a motley collection of cases, boxes, and bundles done up in blue-striped dust-sheets; there was even a crib, packed up with household goods. One chap staggered in, bent double under several mattresses he had brought with him across the Channel in a fishing boat; on realising that he had brought too much, he had intended to leave them in the boat, but they had been unloaded by zealous soldiers helping them ashore in Folkestone.

The refugees were welcomed heartily with the Belgian National Anthem being played on the Meeting House organ and a speech from the Lord Mayor. Once the formalities were out of the way, trays of steaming soup were served along with coffee, bread and cheese, jam and fruit.

Illustration from the Mount Magazine, showing pupils looking after refugees
– With permission of Sarah Shiels.

The girls of The Mount School were delighted to be involved in this humanitarian operation and details of the experience were recorded in the school's *Mount Magazine*. One of the problems they encountered while helping the refugees was the language barrier, as few Belgians spoke English. Some spoke French but many could converse only in their native Flemish. The girls fell back on their smattering of elementary French but the situation was saved by one of the teachers, Miss Ramsay, whose fluent French proved invaluable. Large cauldrons were set up on gas ranges to cope with the piles of dirty crockery, while the refugees made themselves as comfortable as possible. The women and children were provided with makeshift beds in the main Meeting House and the men were split between the cloakrooms and the old library.

Refugees remained at the Meeting House for a brief time before being allocated billets, either in York or the surrounding area. They were popular with those caring for them and the children provided great entertainment. Two donated rocking horses were set up in the yard and were never short of queues of small children; many toys were donated from around the city and handed out to little ones, with penny dolls

Illustration from the Mount Magazine – schoolgirls caring for refugee children – With permission of Sarah Shiels.

being the most popular. One elderly lady begged to be given a penny doll and slept happily with it on her pillow. The girls from The Mount enjoyed their caring duties, but none so much as the opportunity to bath babies and play with the youngsters when they were allowed.

Every effort was made to billet families together and in one case, three generations of the same family were taken in by Mr Seebohm Rowntree, a member of the Rowntree chocolate family and great social philanthropist. There was one particular concern, however, with the integration of refugees into York life: that they might be mistaken for aliens or worse – German spies. It was proposed that all refugees should wear a badge to identify them as such, thereby avoiding the risk of persecution.

By the time the war ended, almost 250,000 Belgian refugees had been welcomed into Britain by communities all over the country and the citizens of York had played their part wholeheartedly.

Zeppelins

York, like many other cities during the war, was coping with fear of invasion and attack on many different levels. First came the insidious fear of the 'enemy within' in the form of non-naturalised Germans, then the overt fear of direct attack by enemy forces by ships at sea or Zeppelin raids. The first enemy attacks on British soil came in

December 1914, injuring and killing civilians and shocking the nation by bringing the perilous nature of modern warfare right to their doorstep.

German warships off the coast of Hartlepool and Scarborough began firing shells at both towns at around 8am on 16 December as people were getting up, breakfasting and preparing for work. Residents grabbed whatever they could carry (even a precious, newly-baked Christmas cake in one case) and fled inland as their cobbled, terraced streets filled with fire and smoke behind them; walls collapsed, roofs fell in and houses were demolished. Over 1,000 shells landed on Hartlepool alone that morning, killing more than a hundred people; not for centuries had an enemy so suddenly and powerfully infiltrated British life.

Recruitment poster showing the shell damage to a house in Scarborough after the German raids in December 1914 – Library of Congress.

So monstrous and unthinkable were these attacks that images of them were used as powerful aids to recruitment. If any man had needed a reason to enlist, this was surely it. One of the most potent images to come out of these attacks was a recruitment poster showing a small girl holding a baby in front of No 2 Wykeham Street, Scarborough, which had been reduced to rubble. The poster's caption reads: 'Men of Britain! Will You Stand This?' Seventy-eight women and children in Scarborough were killed and a further 228 were wounded.

This was only the beginning of German attacks on the British Home Front. The evening of 19 January 1915, saw the first ever air raid attack as two Zeppelins dropped bombs on King's Lynn and Great Yarmouth. Only three people were killed, but it was obvious that attacks of this kind would continue for as long as the country was at war. Zeppelin raids were most frequent along the east coast and in London, but towns and cities throughout Britain brought in a variety of precautions to help prepare for the possibility of attacks from the skies. The most obvious precaution was the introduction of a blackout, because the raids always happened at night and relied on Zeppelin crews being able to see their targets illuminated below.

Blackout restrictions were introduced in York in January 1915, shortly after the Zeppelin raid on King's Lynn. Instructions were issued by the chief constable that shopkeepers in York should stop using lights outside their premises and that all windows should be screened to prevent light escaping. In the event of an air raid alarm, the main electricity and gas supplies to the city would be cut. In April, more formalised restrictions were introduced under the Defence of the Realm (Consolidation) Regulations, with strictly observed penalties for non-compliance. From one hour after sunset to one hour before sunrise, the streets of York descended into inky black obscurity. Illuminated signs, street lamps and public lights were extinguished, motor car headlights were shielded and factory roofs were blacked out.

The novelty of the idea of York swathed in darkness soon wore off as residents faced the reality of travelling around a city with no lights to guide them. Before long there were regular court appearances of people who had refused to turn off or shield their lights, particularly cyclists who relied on their lamps in the absence of any other light. One hazard was the danger posed to both cyclists and pedestrians attempting to cross any of York's bridges, as letters to the *Herald* attest;

without lighting, the likelihood of missing the path and falling down the steps to the river was very high.

In the event of an impending air raid, a warning was sounded by police whistle, or even by football rattle, but it was suspected that Zeppelin pilots were turning off their engines, waiting in silence and using the sounds of whistles and rattles below to help find their bearings. A silent warning system was devised, whereby the residents of York would be warned instead by the gas pressure being raised and lowered several times, causing lights to dim and brighten alternatively.

The citizens of York became accustomed to the periodic raising and lowering of gas lights throughout 1915, yet the urgency of it soon wore thin because York itself was fortunate enough to remain free from attack. This run of good luck came to an abrupt and devastating end during the spring of 1916.

The evening of 2 May 1916 was unremarkable in every way. Young Olive Burton, who lived close to the Fulford Road barracks, remembered her mother going to the Theatre Royal that night to see Offenbach's opera *The Tales of Hoffman*. Her mother recalled the gas lighting being raised and lowered during the performance as a warning of potential danger, before being extinguished altogether. Arthur White, the sixteen-year-old son of a verger at the minster was also there and remembered the performance stoically continuing by candlelight. No one considered for a moment that this time, York itself was to be the target.

At around 9.30pm, a large, sinister shadow hung silently in the night sky on the outskirts of the city. For three whole minutes the pilot waited and watched, taking bearings and planning his path of destruction through the city, before restarting his engines which, according to witnesses, droned loudly and gave off plumes of dense black smoke.

The Zeppelin set off in the direction of Nunthorpe Avenue, close to The Mount School where the girls had leapt out of their beds in response to the raising and lowering of the gas lamps. Unlike the city's older residents, the schoolgirls still found excitement in the suggestion of an air raid. Leaning out of windows, they strained to see evidence of a Zeppelin but, as the school bell rang and the gong was sounded, they all followed the drill and were ushered down to the safety of the

Upper Price Street after the Zeppelin Raid.

basement. The operation was overseen by the indomitable Miss Ramsay, who had 'been in London and knew about Zeppelins'. Student Agnes Smithson vividly recalled the girls playing cards to begin with, but when they heard the frightening sound of 'bangs' and 'thumps' from outside, Miss Ramsay kept them calm by reading to them from John Buchan's *The Thirty-Nine Steps*.

Emily Chapman, an unmarried twenty-eight-year-old resident of Nunthorpe Avenue, could hear the sound of the Zeppelin engines overhead and decided, as did many others, to go outside and witness the spectacle for herself. As she opened her front door and stepped out, a bomb exploded on the street in front of her and a piece of shrapnel sliced into her shoulder, killing her instantly.

The Zeppelin next dropped its bombs on the houses of Upper Price Street, completely demolishing the upper storey of number three, the home of George and Sarah Avison. The two pensioners, asleep in their bed, were killed outright; their bodies were found the following morning in the ruins of their kitchen. From there, the Zeppelin headed north across the city towards Peasholme Green and St Saviour's Place, where another six people were killed; all but one had been walking out in the open, making their way home with no regard for the danger they were in. Ernest Coultash and Benjamin Sharpe, employees of Leethams Flour Mills, were killed by shrapnel while on their way home from work; William Chapelow had his legs blown off as he escorted his wife home from the cinema; Private Leslie Hinson and Corporal Edward Beckett deliberately went outside to watch the Zeppelin pass over and both were killed by shrapnel; sixty-five-year-old Susan Waudby was also killed by a piece of shrapnel smashing through the window of her boarding house.

By the time the Zeppelin had finally passed over York, it had dropped around eighteen bombs, killed nine people, injured a further forty and left a narrow trail of destruction across the city. As the performance of *The Tales of Hoffman* came to an end at the Theatre Royal, the audience began to leave the theatre and were shocked to discover that while they had ignored the familiar air raid warning, York had been hit. The girls of The Mount School went out the following morning to see some of the damage for themselves. Agnes Smithson recalled seeing a damaged house, quite possibly that of George and Sarah Avison or one of their neighbours in Upper Price Street. The house was almost completely demolished: a bed stuck out of the rubble

Zeppelin bombs dropped on York, 1916 – Courtesy of Hugh Murray.

at first floor height and clothes were dangling from a nearby tree.

There were a variety of reactions to the Zeppelin raid of 2 May 1916. Initially, there was a great deal of anger, from the ordinary citizen right the way up to the Lord Mayor himself. The city was unprotected, the air raid patrols had not been active enough and, worst of all, according to reports in the *Herald*, lights had been clearly visible all around the North Eastern Railway carriage works and up to half a mile around York Station. Not only that, but the barracks in the city had also been illuminated. A couple of days after the raid, the York Conservative Association passed a resolution 'protesting against the uncivilized warfare of Zeppelins', and made the point that the lighting of places under government control had aided the Zeppelin.

There was, however, a strong sense of community spirit as the people of York pulled together and, within a few days, had raised almost £400 to help those injured or made homeless by the raid. Archbishop Lang, concerned about the potential damage to the minster, ordered a stained glass window to be removed and put into storage for the duration of the war. Then, of course, there was an entrepreneurial reaction, with the swift development of 'Zepp Alarms'. These could be attached to household gaslight fittings so that when the gas pressure dropped, as it did in an air raid, it would ring a bell to warn anyone in the house who was asleep. Although a good idea, it wasn't much use if the household had already gone to bed and turned off the gas lights. In response to this, volunteer street patrols were organised who would sit up through the night with a gas light left burning and, in the event of a late night air raid, they would run down the street 'knocking people up'.

On more than one occasion, the streets of York were given over to panic and chaos at the hands of over-zealous patrols, who began knocking people up at the merest flicker of the lights. The press carried reports of patrolmen running around 'like maniacs'; of women running barefoot into the street clutching their children; there was even the suggestion that a couple of pregnant women had miscarried as a consequence of being forced out of their homes in a panic.

As time wore on, the fear subsided and more orderly instructions regarding what to do in the event of an air raid were issued. People were told to remain indoors during a raid; to keep away from windows; to shelter either in the basement, under the stairs or against a wall at the very least. They were also advised to prepare a kind of homemade respirator from gauze soaked in washing soda to protect them (in theory) from the hazards of a gas leak. Above all else, they were to shield all lights and were prohibited from raising audible alarms such as bells, buzzers or whistles.

The next Zeppelin attack came on the night of 25 September 1916, but this time York was not as vulnerable as it had been four months earlier. Searchlights and anti-aircraft guns had been installed on higher ground in Acomb, to the west of the city and as Zeppelin L-14 made its steady way across the city, the searchlights found its cumbersome bulk and followed it doggedly, as the AA guns fired. The Zeppelin's attack was almost foiled, as it repeatedly changed course to avoid being hit. The crew managed to drop bombs to the east of the city, causing damage to Holy Trinity Church in Heworth, but little else.

The third and final raid came on 27 November, when two Zeppelins approached the city several hours apart. In both cases, they were picked out by the searchlights and fired upon by the AA guns. The report on this spectacle in the *York Press* suggests that people were still so excited by the Zeppelins that, far from following advice to stay indoors, they stood in the streets and cheered as the Zeppelin was shot at. So intense was the anti-aircraft fire that the Zeppelins retreated, though the first one succeeded in dropping its bombs on Haxby Road, Fountayne Street and Wiggington Road; there was just one injury as a result and no fatalities. The people of York took heart from this success and knew that the raiders could be thwarted if everyone played their part.

The city of York was affected by the war in so many different ways. From the opening days of the conflict, life began to change and the population of the city swelled, at first with men in khaki, then with prisoners of war, who were accepted with surprising tolerance and then again with Belgian refugees, warmly welcomed and provided with temporary homes. The effects of war on the city and on everyday life were unavoidable. The terror of being bombed in your own home and all the necessary precautions to help prevent this became woven into the fabric of daily routine, railed against by some but accepted by most as necessary to survive wartime life.

CHAPTER 3

Who's Absent? Is It You? Conscientious Objection in York

Throughout 1915, the scale of the war in Europe developed beyond all expectation. The Western Front sprawled throughout Belgium and France, while the Eastern Front stretched from the Baltic Sea in the north down to the Carpathian Mountains in the south. Allied troops suffered major losses through a combination of poor strategy and lack of munitions. In April, First Lord of the Admiralty Winston Churchill organised an amphibious attack on the Dardanelles and Gallipoli in Turkey, with the intention of capturing Constantinople and diverting German troops from the Western Front. The plan failed and Allied troops were trapped under Turkish siege for eight months, before finally being evacuated in December. In total, over 67,000 Allied troops lost their lives during that campaign, 40,000 of whom were British soldiers.

On 9 May 1915, a further 11,600 lives were lost in a disastrous offensive at Aubers Ridge; a lack of artillery shells was blamed for the failure. Despite the hasty formation of the Ministry of Munitions, a shortage of shells was once again blamed for the catastrophic failure at Loos in September 1915, with 16,000 dead and another 25,000 wounded. Men were being lost in battle at a greater pace than their replacements could either be recruited or trained.

As the issue of recruitment became increasingly urgent, official recruitment posters began to take a different approach by directly addressing women for the first time. One poster exclaimed: 'WOMEN OF BRITAIN SAY – "<u>GO!</u>"' and depicted a mother, wife and young child, all watching with anxious pride as soldiers marched off to war. Another notice asked 'Is your "Best Boy" wearing Khaki?' and continued: 'If he does not think that you and your country are worth fighting for – do you think he is <u>WORTHY</u> of you?' This attempt by the authorities to emasculate men in the eyes of their womenfolk took a more sinister turn, with the issuing of white feathers to any man not wearing uniform. The first white feathers were reportedly handed out in Folkestone but the practice soon spread across the country; they were often issued indiscriminately by young women looking for mischief, and with little thought for the consequences.

Londoner Frederick Broom, for example, was only fifteen years old when he voluntarily joined the army, having persuaded the recruiting sergeant that he was nineteen. He was involved in the retreat from Mons, the Battle of the Marne and the advance to Ypres, before being invalided back to England at the tender age of sixteen. Gunner Broom was stopped on the street in London by four girls who presented him with three white feathers. The girls didn't believe Frederick's story and continued to bait him as a small crowd gathered to watch. Frederick felt so humiliated that he walked straight into the nearest recruiting office to re-join the army.

Recruitment in York was slow throughout 1915 and frustration among those in authority spilled over into the press. The *Herald* began publishing lists of local men who had enlisted and soldiers were instructed to wear their uniform in public at all times, in the hope of shaming men into joining up. One of the unfortunate consequences of this, however, was that men who contributed to the war effort in a civilian role became the subject of public rancour. The men who worked at the Auxiliary Military Hospital on Haxby Road, for example, at the Ordnance Depot, the NER or for the Army Pay Corps, all fell foul of being labelled 'slackers' and 'shirkers'.

Recruiting officers were beginning to turn a blind eye to minor health issues, height below military standard and poor eyesight, in a bid to increase the numbers of men being accepted into the army. It became apparent that a great many 'short' men were willing to enlist, but were too far below regular army height standards and, as a result,

'Bantam' battalions were formed. To be accepted for the 'Bantams', men had to be between 5 ft and 5 ft 3 ins tall, with a chest measurement of between 33–34 ins. Three men from York, R. S. Parker, J. Howard and T. Middleton, were among the first to join Bantam battalions.

In April 1915, a full scale recruitment campaign took place across the West Riding of Yorkshire, which resulted in 7,036 new recruits – a figure that local land owner the Earl of Harewood called 'a very inadequate result for so thickly populated a county with a population equal to the whole of Wales'. After successfully forming a Pals Battalion Heavy Battery in April 1915, York attempted to form another in October, but by the end of a three-week recruitment drive, only thirty seven out of an estimated 10,000 eligible men had joined up.

York seemed to struggle with recruitment more than other areas of the country and there are a number of possible reasons for this: York had a high Quaker, and therefore pacifist, population; there were a lot of jobs in 'reserved occupations', such as the North Eastern Railway, and also, many jobs in York involved skilled work which paid a better wage than the military.

Slow recruitment was, nonetheless, a national problem and it was only a matter of time before the government were forced to accept that a volunteer army was not going to be adequate to defeat the might of the German Army. The argument in favour of conscription gathered pace during 1915 and the Military Service Act was finally introduced in January of 1916.

Crisis of Conscience

In broad terms, the Military Service Act meant that every unmarried man between the ages of 18 and 41 was

MILITARY SERVICE ACT
1916

EVERY UNMARRIED MAN
of
MILITARY AGE
Not excepted or exempted under this Act
CAN CHOOSE
ONE OF TWO COURSES:
(1) He can ENLIST AT ONCE and join the Colours without delay:
(2) He can ATTEST AT ONCE UNDER THE GROUP SYSTEM and be called up in due course with his Group.

If he does neither, a third course awaits him:
HE WILL BE DEEMED TO HAVE ENLISTED
under the Military Service Act
ON THURSDAY, MARCH 2nd, 1916.
HE WILL BE PLACED IN THE RESERVE, AND BE CALLED UP IN HIS CLASS.
as the Military Authorities may determine.

Poster outlining the Military Service Act 1916 – Library of Congress.

'deemed to have enlisted for the period of the war'. Joining the armed forces was no longer a matter of choice, it was compulsory. Crucially though, a clause was added to the Act making allowances for anyone holding a conscientious objection to combatant service; this historic clause exempted men from joining the army if they could prove they had a sincerely held objection to taking up arms. It did not automatically grant them the right to *absolute* exemption, however. A man who could prove that he held a sincere objection to warfare would be freed from the obligation to fight, but they would still be expected to help the war effort in other ways.

Throughout the war, various types of alternative service were available, including the Friends' Ambulance Unit (FAU), the Royal Army Medical Corps (RAMC), the Non-Combatant Corps (NCC) and various Home Office Work Schemes, which purportedly involved work of 'national importance'. Men who refused to be involved in any of these alternatives were sent to prison.

For the many thousands of men who felt strongly that this war, or indeed any war, was wrong, the Military Service Act presented them with some difficult choices. No longer free to act according to their own will, even if that had meant being labelled a 'shirker', they now had to make an official stand and be prepared to argue their beliefs before sceptical, and sometimes hostile, tribunals.

The implications of the conscientious objection clause were particularly relevant in York because of the city's Quaker population. The outbreak of war in 1914 had taken the country largely by surprise and it was no different for the Society of Friends, or Quakers. Despite pacifism being at the heart of Quakerism, the society was initially divided over how to react to the war; whether to fly in the face of patriotism and hold true to their pacifist principles by condemning the war, or support the decision of the British government to defend the rights of Belgium. At the beginning of the war, the Society of Friends even went as far as issuing a statement recognising that the government had 'made most strenuous efforts to preserve peace' and had 'a grave sense of duty to a smaller State to which we had moral and treaty obligations.'

Accordingly, many Quakers enlisted out of a sense of national duty, while others remained steadfast in their pacifism. The famous Rowntree family of York were all Quakers and they sought to treat everyone, whatever their opinion on the war, with fairness and acceptance. In the early days of the war, Joseph Rowntree pledged to keep open the jobs of any employees wishing to enlist and to ensure that their families were looked after. The Rowntree family were also instrumental in the reception and care of Belgian refugees in York and gave over the newly completed dining block at the Cocoa Works to be used as an auxiliary military hospital.

'Who's Absent? Is it You? Recruitment Poster' – Library of Congress.

The introduction of the Military Service Act caused the male Quaker population of York to consider their position even more seriously, as they decided whether or not to register an official conscientious objection.

Having registered a conscientious objection, an individual would appear before a local tribunal, which would consider the sincerity of their objection. Tribunals were comprised of between five and ten 'upstanding' members of the community, usually all men, and at least one military representative to ensure that no-one got away too lightly.

In February 1916, York City Council argued fiercely about who should be included in the York tribunal, before finally voting on the Lord Mayor, W. A. Forster Todd; Sheriff, C. W. Shipley; Alderman Sir Joseph Sykes Rymer; two members of the Liberal Party, who were also Quakers; and three members of the Labour Party, one of whom was a member of the left-wing Independent Labour Party. There was also, of course, the requisite military representative and two local tradesmen nominated by the Trades Council. It was unusual for a tribunal to include so many members of either the Liberal or Labour Party and this could be why, generally speaking, conscientious objectors were sympathetically treated by the York tribunal, although the questions asked were typically obtuse and often insulting to the individual. It was not unusual, for example, for a man to be asked whether he would stand by and do nothing if a female relative was being attacked.

One Quaker who faced a York tribunal hearing at the Guildhall was Basil Neave, a commercial traveller for Rowntree's. Neave objected to playing any part at all in the war, even to the extent of refusing to join the FAU or the RAMC, because he objected to patching men up and sending them back to fight. The tribunal asserted that many Quakers, who held the same convictions as Neave, *had* joined the FAU and others had enlisted and were fighting. Neave agreed, but argued that it was for each man to act according to his own conscience. Tribunal member Mr Scott then asked the inevitable question: "Should you attempt by any force to protect the chastity of your Sister?" to which Neave replied: "I should hope not". The military representative then asked whether Neave would serve on a minesweeper, where the only purpose was to save lives; he once again replied that he would take no part whatsoever in the war. After appealing against the decision to allow a conditional exemption, Neave was later granted an absolute exemption.

James Leadbetter, a master at Bootham Quaker School in York, was asked by Mr Scott: "Would your conscience allow you to stand by and see three innocent people killed by a rascal without making any attempt to stop him with a revolver or by some other means?" Leadbetter replied: "While I should do my best to otherwise stop him killing before my eyes, I should not kill him." Mr Scott's response was that, in his opinion, Leadbetter would be guilty of murder, or at the very least, accessory to murder. Nonetheless, James Leadbetter had been born a Quaker and the tribunal accepted his claim, granting him an absolute exemption from all military service. It was a similar story for another Bootham man, senior housemaster Charles Hodgson, who was prepared to train men in the FAU, but not willing to undertake military service.

Wilfred Crosland, who worked as a sub-warden at the York Settlement, an adult education institution founded by Liberal MP Arnold Rowntree in York, fared similarly at his tribunal. He was granted an exemption, conditional on him remaining in the same employment. The military representative at this tribunal appealed against the decision, arguing that Crosland was a qualified ambulance man and his skills would be of value. The appeal was overturned because Crosland could prove he had been a Quaker all his life; there was no question of the sincerity of his beliefs.

Attempting to secure an exemption from military service by claiming a conscientious objection was a difficult and often humiliating process. National patriotism and the ardent belief that every man should be doing his bit for King and country meant that anyone appearing to shirk their duty faced being publicly berated, privately shunned and even subjected to physical attack. Although men dealt with the consequences of their decisions differently, depending on the outcome of their tribunal hearings, the options available to them were limited.

Many conscientious objections were on political, rather than religious grounds and Fred Bradley, a 40-year-old clerk at Rowntree's, was one such objector. Bradley was a socialist who believed that the government had no right to rob him of his free will and that he, as a working man, had no feud with the working men of Germany. Bradley was also a member of the No Conscription Fellowship (NCF), an organisation founded in late 1914 to campaign against the introduction of conscription. When conscription was introduced in 1916, the NCF concentrated its efforts instead on supporting and advising conscientious objectors.

While tribunals had some sympathy with an objection on religious grounds, they generally had little time for political objections but, because Bradley had been a member of the NCF from the beginning, there was little room to doubt the sincerity of his claim. Bradley was granted a partial exemption, which meant he was expected to take up non-combatant duties with the Non-Combatant Corps. Bradley, like most political objectors, refused any involvement whatsoever that would aid the furtherance of the war, so he simply failed to report for duty.

He was subsequently arrested and appeared in court on 29 June 1916, charged with failing to abide by the laws of the land. Bradley argued his case eloquently, stating that though he may perhaps be a 'fanatic', he was certainly no coward and would refuse to obey a single order if he were forced to join the army. Bradley was commended for his principles by one of the magistrates, retired labour politician A. P. Mawson, who nonetheless had no option but to hand him over to the authorities. Bradley remained true to his word and from the outset refused to wear khaki or to follow a single military order.

Another magistrate who publicly expressed his sympathy for the lot of York's conscientious objectors was Robert Kay, headmaster of Park Grove School. Kay was particularly vocal in the cases of twenty-one-year-old Richie Henderson of Vyner Street (another Rowntree's employee) and twenty-four-year-old Harold Deighton of Fenwick Street. Both men had objected on political grounds and, like Fred Bradley, were awarded partial exemptions and ordered to report for duty with the Non-Combatant Corps. Like Bradley, they too were arrested for failing to turn up and appeared in court on 22 May. Richie Henderson stated that he was not there to 'save his skin' but to: 'oppose the present military system which threaten[s] to make slaves of the future generations. It [is] the liberty of the individual to act according to the dictates of conscience as to what was right and what was wrong in the matter of life and death'. He went on to express his admiration for the heroic soldiers who were giving up their lives for a cause they believed in, but concluded that: 'the Court would never make [me] depart from the principles which [I] believe to be right, and for which [I am] willing to stand up to the end'.

Robert Kay did what was legally expected of him: he found the men guilty and handed them over to the military authorities, but not before he had expressed his own opinion. He stated that he 'was very much in sympathy' with Richie Henderson and that, in his opinion, it had taken much courage to say and do what Henderson had done.

Both Henderson and Deighton were taken to Fulford Barracks where, as they refused to follow military orders and would neither prepare nor wear any of their kit, they were consequently charged with insubordination, court martialled and sentenced to twenty-eight days' confinement. Upon release, the men still refused to follow orders and the process was repeated again and again, as was common practice with conscientious objectors who took this stand.

When twenty-seven-year-old Herbert Coupland, an education clerk and resident of Skeldergate, appeared in court in June for failing to respond to his call-up, Robert Kay's frustration with the system could be contained no longer and he spoke out in the *York Press* about the apparent unfairness being perpetrated by tribunals. Some of the men appearing before him in court, he began, had been known to him for many years and were honest, hard-working men who could substantiate their claims. Not shirkers, not slackers, but genuine conscientious objectors.

It was also the case, he continued, that COs with an appeal hearing still pending were being arrested and brought to court. The tribunals, he argued, were not always carrying out their duty, but allowing personal opinion and prejudice to cloud their judgement. Herbert Coupland was one such man and Kay was so incensed by what he considered to be the tribunal's error of judgement, that he refused to hand Coupland over to the military and dismissed the case, allowing Coupland to go free.

His bold actions prompted outrage and the *Herald* demanded Kay be dismissed for wilfully refusing to abide by the law. Coupland was re-arrested and brought before a fresh bench the following day, who were more than prepared to make their feelings clear about the whole debacle. Coupland was told that most people would consider him incredibly selfish, willing to take all the benefits offered by his country but unwilling to give anything in return. Coupland asked for the case to be adjourned because he didn't believe he could be tried for the same offence twice. His request was refused and he was told: 'You are a soldier. We have no sympathy for you.' The bench fined him 40 shillings and handed him over to the waiting military escort. Coupland went before the army medical board on 20 July, 1916 and was found unfit for service.

Despite the unease among some about the efficacy of the tribunals, general opinion still swung against conscientious objectors among both the public and the military. Letters denigrating the men who appeared before tribunals or in court were printed regularly in the press. When five COs appeared in court for the same reasons as Herbert Coupland, in June of 1916, York was still reeling from its first Zeppelin raid, and feelings were running particularly high. While spiteful letters quoting the Bible and upbraiding the COs littered the pages of the local press, one of the five COs concerned found himself in very serious trouble. Andrews Britan, a Quaker and teacher at Park Grove School, had been handed over to the military after his court hearing and, as others before him had done, he refused to don a uniform or follow orders. However, the authorities were determined not to let the COs get the better of them any longer and set about trying to break down Britan's resolve.

Forcibly dressed in uniform, Britan was shackled and transported to Richmond Castle in the North Riding of Yorkshire on Monday, 12 June. He refused to obey an order and was immediately punched in the face by an NCO, leaving him cut and bruised. The following morning, he refused an order to go out on parade and was punched again several times, until he fell to the ground. Two NCOs picked him up and carried him out to the parade ground. Having recovered himself, Britan's determination remained unshaken. He started to explain his position to the commanding officer and began unbuttoning his tunic, saying he could not, in all conscience, wear a military uniform. The captain's response to this was to have Britan stripped down to his underclothes and tied up against a wall in the public square of Richmond Castle, where passers-by could berate and verbally abuse him.

'The Conscientious Objector at the Front'. Cartoon portraying conscientious objectors as cowardly and effeminate.

Britan was placed there as a warning to other potential 'cowards', so when one young man doffed his hat and engaged Britan in conversation he too was promptly arrested. Britan, along with other COs held at Richmond Castle, spent most of his time locked in solitary confinement in an 8ft by 5ft cell, with nothing by way of comfort and one tiny square window, too high to see through. The graffiti left on the cell walls by these men can still be seen today.

The treatment of Andrews Britan was representative of the many conscientious objectors who took this absolutist stance. Treated with shocking brutality, COs faced being regularly beaten, stripped, publicly humiliated and fed on bread and water rations; ordeals which often lasted for weeks. For some though, even worse was to come. Britan and his fellow COs at Richmond Castle were told that they were about to shipped out to France, where they would be on 'active service' in a war zone and where the consequences of failing to obey orders carried a far more serious penalty than imprisonment.

Britan, it seems, escaped this particular threat, but sixteen of his peers from Richmond Castle, including fellow York man and Rowntree's clerk Alfred Martlew, were not so fortunate. Shipped to France under cloak of darkness, unable to tell their friends or family what was happening, the 'Richmond Sixteen', as they became known, along with twenty other COs from around the country, were subject to an ever-worsening, ever more frightening punishment regime, before finally being faced with the threat of the death penalty. The treatment of these men was so extreme that some never recovered, either physically or psychological. Alfred Martlew was so affected by his experience that he drowned himself in the River Ouse in 1917.

The experiences of Andrews Britan in particular caused uproar in the local press. Samuel Henry Davies, former Liberal councillor and chemist at Rowntree's, was well-known locally for his work with the No Conscription Fellowship and support for York's conscientious objectors. Determined to expose Britan's ordeal at the hands of the military, Davies gathered independent testimonies and wrote to the *York Press* with his findings. His claims were supported by Arthur Dearlove, a member of the Independent Labour Party, who provided a list of other COs subjected to similar acts of brutality. The many responses were typically divisive. A lot of correspondents, mostly anonymous, argued that Britan had got exactly what he deserved, that he was a 'clown' and a disgrace to his country and that, if anything, he had got off lightly.

Others, including the doyenne of conservative York society, Edith Milner, didn't actually condone the abuse, but instead refused to believe that such a thing was possible and accused Davies of fabricating the whole affair to stir up trouble. Despite being presented with eyewitness accounts of Britan's ordeal, Milner persisted in her views and ended by stating 'there is only one opinion of Britan, he is a coward.' Fred Bradley, himself a CO about to appear in court for refusing to answer to his call-up, responded by writing that anyone who knew Milner wouldn't be the least bit surprised by her avowed refusal to believe the facts before her, if they differed from her own view.

While attitudes towards conscientious objection altered little throughout the war, the increasing exposure of instances of abuse and ill-treatment resulted in a growing determination that the men concerned should at least be treated fairly. Individual cases of abuse were frequently raised in Parliament; the definition of the conscientious objection clause was clarified and all its implications provided for. Although men like Andrews Britan had to accept they would feel the full force of the law for their absolutist position, they deserved the right to act according to their conscience without fear of physical harm.

Corder Catchpool – Unlikely Hero

Bootham School in York is a Quaker establishment and had strong links to the pacifist movement during the First World War, with schoolmasters of fighting age applying for exemption to military service on grounds of conscience. Although some students went on to enlist, others also adopted a pacifist position and became conscientious objectors. One such student was Corder Catchpool, who attended Bootham from 1900 – 1902. Although he was not a resident of York by the time of the war, the account of his wartime experiences, recorded in the *Bootham School Magazine* is worth mentioning here as an example of the complexities of conscientious objection.

Towards the end of 1914, an entirely voluntary relief service was founded by Quaker Philip Baker to provide emergency medical aid to soldiers in Belgium. The First Anglo-Belgian Ambulance Service, which later became more famously known as the Friends' Ambulance Unit, set sail for Dunkirk at the end of October. The unit comprised of forty-three men, one of whom was Corder Catchpool.

The events recorded in the *Bootham School Magazine* are based on an extract of a letter dated 30 April 1915, written by Catchpool while he was serving with the FAU near Ypres. He was experiencing his first period of calm after eight days in the midst of furious fighting. Catchpool wrote his letter while sitting in the garden of the College of St Stanislas, where his unit had been billeted for the previous five months. That first evening of peace seemed 'infinitely sweet' after the 'awful turmoil, the bodily fatigue and the mental strain' of the previous eight days, during which time he had not once removed either his jacket or boots, let alone slept.

Catchpool described passing by the ruined city of Ypres and seeing its rubble being shelled afresh by German siege guns. As his ambulance headed towards the reserve trenches, the surrounding villages were being used as target practice and the air was heavy with acrid smoke. When the message came that the Germans had 'broken through', the ambulances headed past the reserve trenches and were met by staggering columns of gassed men 'choking, gasping, dying, asphyxiated'. Throughout the night the FAU travelled the 8 kilometres to the rail head and back several times, taking as many men as they could move. German troops gained ground to within 3 kilometres of the village where ambulances were picking up the wounded.

The battle raged for five days without any let up. Wounded men continued to pour into the village and were transported to safety by the FAU, until one driver was injured and two ambulances were damaged by shell fire. The rail head had also come under shell fire and the ambulance journeys were becoming increasingly perilous. At one stage, the lanes were blocked by piles of earth thrown up by exploding shells; Catchpool, along with the other FAU drivers and orderlies, moved the earth with their hands and feet to clear the way, before driving carefully over the debris.

When the wing of a civilian hospital took a direct hit, Catchpool was among the first on the scene to find the bodies of eleven nuns strewn about, along with elderly men and women, children and invalids lying bleeding in their beds, all coated in fine, white plaster dust from the collapsed ceiling.

Throughout these long, traumatic days, the FAU did much more than just attend to the wounds of soldiers and civilians; in the quieter moments, they set up kitchens to serve tea, hot OXO, cocoa, biscuits and chocolates, even when under fire. At one point, the kitchen car was riddled with bullet holes, but 'no vital part [was] touched except the OXO boiler', which had several holes and could only be 'half filled'.

Corder Catchpool.

These astonishing experiences took place over little more than a week and represent a mere thumbnail sketch of Catchpool's career with the FAU. Often putting himself in extreme danger in order to save lives rather than take them, Catchpool qualified for the Mons Star medal.

When conscription was introduced in 1916, Catchpool chose to leave the FAU and his reasoning for this decision is complex, but gives an insight into what drove the consciences of some of these men. With the introduction of conscription, more Friends were joining the FAU than ever before as an 'alternative' to military service. This meant the FAU was no longer a 'voluntary' unit in the truest sense of the word; 'volunteers' were not free to act entirely according to their conscience, rather they were being 'forced' into the least compromising alternative. Catchpool felt that the men joining the FAU after conscription were entering into a kind of bargain with militarism, something he had never been prepared to do. Catchpool left the FAU and his exemption from military service was immediately revoked; he took an absolutist position, which resulted in him being sent to prison no fewer than four times in the remaining two years of the war.

After the war, Catchpool became involved in war victims relief work in Germany and in 1931, he was appointed Quaker Representative to the Quaker Centre in Berlin, where he offered advice to pacifists facing persecution. In 1933, Catchpool defied Nazi Party orders for German citizens to boycott shops owned by Jews, was arrested and interrogated for thirty-six hours by the Gestapo. He returned to Britain in 1936 and supported conscientious objectors during the Second World War.

Exemption, Suspicion and Conspiracy

Conscientious objection was not the only grounds for exemption from military service; men could also apply for exemption if they were employed in work that was 'expedient to the National interests' or if, by joining the army, they would leave their family or business in financial hardship or, quite simply, they were medically unfit. It was not uncommon for business owners to request exemption on behalf of their workers. Those in positions of authority and influence faced controversy and allegations of treachery when they sought exemptions for others and this was no different for the Rowntree family.

Despite Rowntree's Cocoa Works pledging to support the families of enlisted employees and reserving their jobs, the Rowntree family were never far away from accusations of being pro-German. This may have stemmed from the German ancestry of Seebohm Rowntree, but the family's pacifist beliefs meant that suspicion was always bubbling away, beneath a veneer of politeness.

When Arnold Rowntree's wife, May, gave a lecture to the York Settlement in January 1915, rather than blame Germany's invasion of

Belgium as the cause of war, she asserted that the war 'was the result of wrong thinking on the part of all the nations involved, and we were in it just as much as any other'. The press interpreted this as suggesting that Britain was as responsible for the war as Germany, leading the *Herald* to attack the Rowntrees, and Quakers in general, for their 'far-fetched theories and explanations to avoid attributing the war to its real and only cause, German greed and aggression'.

After the introduction of conscription, Seebohm Rowntree did the family name no favours when he applied for exemption from military service for five of his personal employees. Three of the men were gardeners, working on a project to revive York's once flourishing chicory growing industry. Despite being in the early stages, the project had the backing of the Board of Agriculture, with the potential to be extremely lucrative and a benefit to the local economy, but as the men worked in the garden of Seebohm's private residence, it must have looked as though he was simply preserving his own lifestyle. Another of the men was a coachman who, at forty, was close to the upper limit of 'fighting age' anyway; Seebohm argued that his wife was ill and he could not manage without the services of a reliable coachman. The final claim was for his private secretary, who assisted him in his work for the Welfare Department of the Ministry of Munitions.

In addition to exemption applications for personal employees, the Rowntrees also had a reputation for applying for exemptions for many of their staff at the Cocoa Works. The company was a major employer in York and the management was determined to keep production running throughout the war – no easy feat when the workforce is being steadily and continually depleted by the war. Rowntree's installed new, labour-saving machinery to mitigate their dwindling skill base, but still needed to hold on to as many skilled workers as possible. They regularly applied for exemptions for 'indispensable' members of the workforce and, although they were able to support and justify the claims at tribunal, it did not stop the bandying of accusations and development of conspiracy theories in the community.

It was propounded that Rowntree's, to support their 'pro-German', pacifist agenda, would entice men to work for them, on the understanding that Rowntree's would then 'secure' exemption for these men. Beyond the occasional employee who had lied to Rowntree's about his age or health in order gain employment, there was no evidence whatsoever for this charge, but letters on the subject appeared regularly in the *Press* and *Herald.* It was suggested by one contributor that the tribunals should closely scrutinise lists of all employees considered 'indispensable' by Rowntree's, so that the outrageous scandal could be brought to an end.

Whatever the politics surrounding conscription, its effects on the people of York were long lasting. Those who went to fight were hailed as heroes, those who chose not to were often labelled cowards. The division of opinion lasted far longer than the war itself, as every institution commemorated their fallen heroes, but chose to forget men like Alfred Martlew and Andrews Britan.

CHAPTER 4

The Cocoa Works

York is famous for many things, but perhaps most notably for being the birthplace of Rowntree & Co. Much loved British confectionary like Fruit Pastilles, Kit Kat and Polo mints all originated in York. The history of Rowntree's can be traced back to 1725, when a Quaker woman, Mary Tuke, opened a small grocery shop in the Walmgate area of the city; by the 1780s the shop had expanded to include a range of teas and coffees, as well as hot chocolate drinks that were bought in ready made. The chocolate drinks became such a popular part of the range that, in 1785, the business, now being run by Mary's grandson William, began manufacturing cocoa and chocolate at a site on Coppergate. By the mid-nineteenth century, the cocoa and chocolate manufacturing side of the business was thriving and it was purchased in 1862 by company employee and Quaker, Henry Isaac Rowntree. Henry was joined in business by his brother Joseph in 1869 and together they set about building the foundations of the Rowntree's empire.

From humble beginnings, with a dozen employees and a ramshackle factory on the site of a disused foundry at Tanners Moat, H. I. Rowntree & Co innovated and expanded. Despite Henry's untimely death in 1883, Rowntree's continued to thrive under Joseph's leadership and by 1906 the company occupied a modern, purpose built factory on a twenty-four acre site off Haxby Road, employing over 4,000 workers. Their most popular products were Fruit Pastilles and Rowntree's Elect Cocoa, which was renowned for being 'more than a drink, a food'.

Rowntree & Co was no ordinary employer though, and Joseph

Rowntree was no ordinary businessman. While determined to produce top quality chocolate and confectionery, he was equally resolved to look after the welfare of his workforce and the Cocoa Works on Haxby Road was designed to be much more than just a workplace. Joseph Rowntree built a dining block for his workers and a gymnasium for fitness and recreation, provided health care, ran savings schemes and pension plans, employed welfare officers to attend to workers' personal problems and even offered a property in Scarborough where workers could convalesce after illness.

Rowntree's also promoted a range of social activities by encouraging team sports, providing allotments and organising outings, parties and competitions. In 1909, Joseph Rowntree commissioned the construction of the Yearsley Baths, an open air swimming baths across the road from the Cocoa Works for the use of all York citizens. Just five years before, Joseph had given around half of his wealth to set up three charitable trusts intended to alleviate the causes of poverty. The Joseph Rowntree Foundation still exists today and works to improve the social conditions of the most vulnerable members of society throughout the UK.

The *Cocoa Works Magazine*

Founded in 1902, the *Cocoa Works Magazine* (*CWM*) became a regular feature of working life at Rowntree's. Its purpose was to maintain communication between management and the workforce and it provides a fascinating glimpse into daily life at this unique organisation. Traditionally, each issue began with an editorial by Joseph Rowntree himself; he was clearly a highly respected figurehead, who addressed his workforce with a kind of paternal affection. He discussed events since the previous issue, informed the workforce of developments at the Cocoa Works and praised employees' achievements. His tone was always warm and appreciative, even when dealing with the harsh realities of life, none harsher than the effects of war.

The first wartime edition of the *CWM* was published in December 1914 and the opening address by Joseph Rowntree was more sombre than usual. He began by referring to the 500 men who had already left the Cocoa Works and were wearing khaki in various parts of Europe, referring with particular sadness to the two employees who had already been killed in action: H. S. Wadsworth of the Melangeur Department,

*Christmas 1914 Rowntree's tin sent to all York men serving overseas –
Courtesy of York Cocoa House.*

lost at the Battle of the Aisne and W. McLellan of the Gum Department,
lost at the Battle of the Marne. It was a *CWM* convention to always
refer to employees by name, then department and this must have
created a strong sense of belonging among workers as the war
progressed and the magazine became increasingly filled with news of
the injured and fallen. Even if readers did not recognise a name, they
would have known his department and felt the loss more keenly.

When Joseph Rowntree wrote that first wartime editorial, he would
have had no idea just how many more times he would have to write,
with increasing sadness, of wounded, missing or killed employees; but
write he did and every single man had his place within the pages of the
CWM.

By December 1915 there were over 1,000 Rowntree's employees
serving with the armed forces, plus 300 temporary staff. Sixteen men
had been killed in action, five were missing, nine were prisoners of
war and many more had been wounded. The following December, the
number of dead rose to fifty, more than tripling in a year, mainly due
to the July-November Somme offensive. By the end of 1917, the
situation had worsened still further; the total number of serving
employees had risen to a staggering 2,724, with 107 men killed by
'wounds, disease, drowning or accident'.

Finally, in the Christmas 1918 issue, the Cocoa Works staff were able to put behind them four years of 'sorrow, suffering, and sacrifice [which had] been a denial of the spirit and the message of Christmas'. Joseph Rowntree rejoiced to think that the factory would soon have the pleasure of welcoming home the men who had been fighting for their country. Throughout the war, Joseph Rowntree was always careful to express his gratitude to the remaining workforce for showing great spirit and coping with straitened times and an increased workload. The staff even lost their new dining block to the war effort, when 1,000 men of the 8th Battalion, West Yorkshire Regiment (Territorials) were quartered there during the opening months of the conflict, departing for Flanders in late February 1915. Joseph Rowntree had been so impressed with the battalion during their time at the Cocoa Works, that he wrote to its commanding officer to express his appreciation for the 'very pleasant and cordial relations' which had existed between all concerned.

The *CWM* didn't exist solely to pass on sad news though; it also needed to boost morale, share hopes and aspirations for the future and encourage the workforce to pull together and remain productive. Rowntree's distributed the magazine to every employee, whether they were working at the Cocoa Works in York, at any of the national depots or serving overseas. The Cocoa Works was as much about community as employment, and Joseph Rowntree wanted every worker to feel a valued member of the team, particularly those who were far from home and facing untold danger. In the December 1916 issue, a plea to the 'Cocoa Boys in khaki' was printed, urging them to notify Rowntree's Social Department of any change in regimental address. 'We have endeavoured to keep in touch,' it went on, 'to send you the *CWM* and parcels of cocoa, chocolate and winter comforts, some of these parcels have been returned to us and if your home address in our records is obsolete, we lose touch with you completely. We want you to know that, though temporarily absent, the old Firm has not forgotten you.'

This sense of community sometimes extended beyond the walls of the Cocoa Works. Rowntree's, in conjunction with Mayor John Bowes Morrell and Sheriff Oscar F. Rowntree, designed and produced special tins of chocolate, which were sent out to every York man in the armed forces at Christmas 1914. The inscription on the lid read:

The Lord Mayor of York John Bowes Morrell and the Sheriff Oscar F Rowntree send best wishes for a happy Christmas and a bright New Year to all York men who are serving their King and Country, Christmas 1914.

Around 250 men wrote to thank the Lord Mayor and Sheriff for their tin and their letters show what an impact the gift had on those who received them. It was a little piece of home, a token that showed they were being remembered with pride; naturally though, the tins also sparked envy among comrades who were not fortunate enough to hail from York.

The sense of community at Rowntree's was never felt more keenly than when a man on active service in some far-flung part of the world miraculously bumped into another man from the Cocoa Works. H. Groves of the Almond Paste department was so pleased to meet up with another man from the 'old Firm', that they greeted each other with such delight, 'you would have thought peace had been declared'.

The men also wrote in when they saw Rowntree's advertising boards in the most unlikely of locations throughout France or Belgium or, even better, when they spotted a Rowntree's tin being put to an unexpected use. T. Pearson from Packing saw a man having a wash in a 4lb clear gum tin near the Front Lines and H. Whiteley from the Offices admitted using one as a 'gas gong' to warn of impending gas attack. Albert Hill from the Gum Department wrote from Greece that he had seen a small gum tin being used as a cigarette case by a Turkish prisoner.

Philanthropy

Integral to the ethos of the Rowntree family was concern for others. Throughout the war, inspired by the philanthropy of Joseph Rowntree, Cocoa Works employees were actively involved in various collections to provide help and respite for the lads serving overseas, for wounded soldiers and for the Belgian refugees fleeing from atrocities in their own country.

During the autumn and winter of 1914, the people of York had ensured that Belgian refugees were given a warm welcome and at the heart of this relief work were the Quaker community and, therefore, the Rowntree family. The Cocoa Works organised a relief fund to pay for the billeting of refugees, on a temporary basis to begin with, but providing homes for them in the long term. The *CWM* printed a list of funds raised by each department at the end of December which, incidentally, gives an insight into wages and company hierarchy. The office staff at the top end of the scale, for example, contributed an impressive £27 12s 10d (worth almost £2,700 today, based on RPI inflation) between them, followed by the Cream Covering Dept who collected £12 0s 9d (£1,175 today) and the Almond Paste Dept with £11 11s 5d (£1,130 today). At the bottom end of the scale were the Labourers and the Stables who, despite being the lowest paid workers in the company, still contributed 6s 12d (£34) and 4s 8d (£23) respectively. By the end of December 1914, the total amount raised by Rowntree's was £167 15s 10d (approximately £16,400 today).

This money was used to secure housing fit for families in New Earswick, a model village in York established by Joseph Rowntree, following Seebhom Rowntree's 1901 report *Poverty: a study of town life*. Joseph was so appalled by the extent of the overcrowded, insanitary and squalid living conditions revealed by the report, that he committed to providing a high standard of housing at an affordable price for working men and women. The homes were light, spacious and each had a garden with a fruit tree. It was to New Earswick that the Belgian families came and the money raised by Rowntree's staff was used to furnish the empty homes. Everything was supplied for those who had left their own homes with nothing, along with grants for Belgian families who needed extra financial support. Joseph Rowntree thanked the ladies who had taken charge of the project:

Hats off to the ladies who took possession of these houses into which furniture and pots and pans, linoleum and pictures, crockery and bedding had been dumped down, by mere men, and with soap and water and needle and thread and womanly taste and skill, turned chaos into beauty.

Despite the casual misogyny implying that women are at their best when making a home, the gratitude for their work is apparent and the sense of community spirit is heartening. The collective effort did not end there though; the Belgian Relief Fund continued and by May 1915 a staggering £308 12s 11½d (roughly £30,152 today) had been raised,

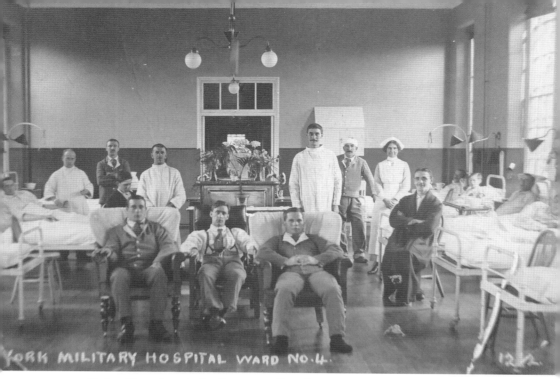

York military hospital – Courtesy of Hugh Murray.

enabling fifty-six refugees to be housed. Although donations naturally began to tail off (particularly after the founding of the Wounded Soldiers Fund), by the end of 1915, almost seventy refugees had found homes, with most of these households soon becoming self-supporting. This sometimes meant a highly skilled refugee taking a labouring job, rather than continuing to rely on charity; but in families where the head of the house was unable to work, assistance was still provided by the Relief fund.

Not satisfied with providing help for Belgian refugees, staff at the Cocoa Works set up all manner of other collections to send gifts to friends and colleagues at war. The Wounded Soldiers Fund was started in September 1915, shortly after the company gave up its new dining block for use as a military hospital. This fund aimed simply to bring some happiness to men stranded in hospitals, often far from their homes and families. When it came to their own employees, Rowntree's took this duty particularly seriously. When the company got word of a 'Cocoa Boy' shipped back to a hospital far from home, they would send his details to the nearest Travelling Depot or Outside Advertising Staff, who would then arrange to visit him. If possible, a member of the man's family would be invited to stay with these employees, so that they too could visit.

The fund provided wounded men with: tobacco, cigarettes, pipes, matches, fruit, writing pads and envelopes, postage stamps, brush & comb bags, soap and, of course, chocolate and gums. The Packing and Stores Department alone raised enough to supply 1,000 packs of woodbines and a considerable quantity of tobacco, pipes, matches, fruit and biscuits. This generosity extended further than the auxiliary hospital at the Cocoa Works Dining Block to the other military hospitals on Fulford Road and St Oswald's Road, and ensured that wounded 'Cocoa Boys' at other hospitals around the country received weekly parcels of chocolate and cigarettes. It even paid for free accommodation for impoverished relatives visiting men at the Haxby Road hospital.

On Christmas morning 1916, every wounded soldier in York woke to find a 'neat little box on his locker', containing shaving soap, cigars, matches and chocolate and bearing the inscription 'With the Compliments of Messrs Rowntree's Employees'. The whole scheme had been carefully planned to be a surprise; the nursing staff had waited until all the patients were asleep before depositing the boxes on the lockers.

By 1917, there were so many wounded soldiers in York that they had become a regular part of city life, with weekly concerts being given at the various hospitals and 'Cocoa Girls' being organised into visiting parties to ensure that every man would receive a visitor. In July that year, Joseph Rowntree held a garden party and concert in honour of York's wounded soldiers in the grounds of the Cocoa Works. Every wounded man then recovering in a York hospital and well enough to attend was invited, along with factory employees; all were welcomed with a speech by Joseph Rowntree's nephew, the Liberal MP Arnold Rowntree.

In addition to the company-wide fundraising effort, individual departments also organised special local collections for their own workmates. In the last few months of 1915, for example, the Almond Paste Department (4th floor) subscribed for many weeks to provide each of the fourteen men from the Paste Department serving at the front with a Christmas parcel containing the following:

1 pair mittens
2 pocket handkerchiefs
4 packets Gold Flake
12 boxes matches
1 box butterscotch
2 boxes chocolate

Each parcel included a letter, which read:

Dear Friend,
Your work mates are often thinking about you, and therefore desire to express their feelings for the work you are doing for the Empire.
As a reminder of this thought they are sending you a small parcel with the very best wishes for your good health and safe return.

Paramount in the hearts and minds of Cocoa Works employees was the wish that their colleagues should not be forgotten and, importantly, should *know* that they were not forgotten. The effect of these messages and gifts from home on the morale of York men either fighting or wounded, can not be underestimated. It is a powerful thing to know that you still belong somewhere when the world is blowing up around your ears.

War Savings

In a bid to reduce the level of borrowing and to raise funds to support the war effort, the British government started a National Savings movement in 1916. The people of Britain were encouraged to invest their money in bonds, certificates and savings stamps. The government would use this money to purchase artillery, munitions and tanks; then, after the war, investors could cash in their bonds with interest. National Savings were billed as just about the most patriotic measure a civilian could take: loaning their own hard-earned money to help their country defeat the enemy. Savings groups were quickly established in factories, offices and clubs throughout the country and Rowntree's was no different.

The Rowntree's Employees War Savings Association was formed on 13 July, 1916 and its intention was clear:

to assist the government to borrow money by providing a system whereby the savings of its members in sums of sixpence upwards can be collected with a minimum of trouble to them. The money is required to provide guns, shells, aircraft etc. The need is URGENT.

Anyone participating in the scheme could expect to accrue interest at 5.25 per cent per annum, so for every 15s 6d (around £57) invested, the government would repay 20s (£75 today) in five years.

The importance of taking part in the War Savings Association was laid out for employees in this powerful statement:

The War can be won, well won, and more quickly won, if behind the firing line the people at home stand and offer their money to their country. Money cannot be used more patriotically.

- *Join the financial army without delay and take YOUR part in the WAR. Everyone's effort counts.*
- *Every sixpence saved helps twice, first when you don't spend it and again when you lend it to the nation.*
- *When you spend you make things dearer for everyone, especially for those who are poorer than you.*
- *SAVE AND HELP TO WIN VICTORY AND PEACE.*

More money meant more guns, shells, ships and aircraft leading to a speedier and more complete victory. The message obviously hit home because between the inception of the Rowntree's Employees War Savings Association in July 1916 and September 1917, it had purchased 5,113 £1 certificates (worth over £300,000 today) and topped the list of 115 similar associations in York both in terms of membership and contributions. The Cocoa Works War Savings Association was finally closed in the spring of 1919; at its peak, membership had reached 1,400, and it had purchased a total of 8,717 £1 certificates.

Social Life

The Cocoa Works had an active and well organised programme of social and sporting events to keep workers occupied in their spare time.

Lady gardeners at Rowntree's during wartime – © Nestlé UK & Ireland Archive.

Before the war, team sporting events were a prominent fixture in the Cocoa Works calendar, with football, cricket and hockey being the most popular. During the war, every attempt was made to keep factory sports alive, but it became increasingly difficult to put together half-decent teams. It was commonplace for team managers to spend their Friday nights frantically calling at the houses of workers, trying to collect a team for the next day's match. Quite often, men who had played on the previous Saturday had disappeared into the army before the next match. As the football season drew to a close in the spring of 1916, the *Cocoa Works Magazine* reported that the season had started well enough but, thanks largely to the introduction of conscription halfway through the season, it had become something of a 'dead-letter' after the first three matches.

A consequence of the dwindling number of male workers was the increase in number of female workers and this was reflected in their increased involvement in sport. A girls' hockey club had been formed in 1911, followed by a girls' cricket club in 1913, but participation by female workers was on a much smaller scale than the men's clubs. Though the men's football, hockey and cricket clubs had several teams and an established inter-departmental competition, the women had few teams and no such competition. The Girls' Hockey Club had thirty members by its second season, but still only one team represented the

Cocoa Works and competed against ten other girls' hockey teams in the York area.

Prior to the war, girls had been encouraged to take part in less taxing activities more 'suited' to their gender, such as gymnastics, dancing, cookery, dressmaking and hygiene. During the war, participation of women in team sports increased, although they were still treated as something of a novelty by management, as one report of a cricket match during the summer of 1917 attests. The Girls' Cricket Eleven 'smilingly' attended extra practice on a Tuesday night, but their victories were 'not numerous yet'. They did have some success it seems, after the Eleven taught their captain how to bat during a match against St Lawrence Girls.

Another area where women were making their presence felt was in the Cocoa Works allotments. Rowntree's had always given over plots of land for use as allotments by employees, but traditionally these had been used by men, with the physical labour of gardening not deemed a fitting pastime for women. During the First World War, the use of allotments became more important than ever before, particularly with the rising cost of food. Anything that could be home-grown helped the household income go a bit further and defied the efforts of German U-boats to starve Britons by the sinking of merchant ships.

By May 1915, demand for Rowntree's allotments was so great that any 'lads' holding two or more plots were being asked to surrender their extra plots. During 1917, Rowntree's made a further 345 square yards of land available and, for the first time, allowed women to rent allotment space. Anyone renting an allotment was asked to be 'patriotic and wise' by producing as much food from their little space as possible. They were asked to work like they had never worked before and to share the burden with a friend, if it proved too much for them alone. To encourage the growing of fruit and vegetables in place of flowers, the Directors offered a prize for the best 'utilitarian' garden where tidiness and 'clean cultivation' counted for everything. The factory magazine had always offered helpful tips and advice to gardeners on how to get the most from their plots, but this became even more prominent during the war years and there were regular tips on topics such as which variety of potato to grow in different soil types and which type would succeed year after year.

By July 1917, the 'War Gardens', as the extra space had been named, were thriving and the Directors marvelled at the level of commitment which had transformed an empty meadow into a wealth of edible produce. They particularly praised the ladies who had taken up allotments because they had had 'everything to learn', but soon picked up the essentials and 'generally made a very successful show'. A 'Ladies Section' was introduced into the prize-giving and a photograph of some of the proud ladies appeared in the *Cocoa Works Magazine* above the entertaining caption, 'The Almond Paste and Office Girls defy the German Submarines.'

By the end of the war, the ladies' allotments had become just as popular as the men's and there could be no question of going back, even with the high number of men returning to work after demobilisation. Instead, the firm made yet more land available, with a whole swathe being set aside specifically as 'girls' gardens'. At the end of summer 1919, the girls held their own produce show at the Rose Garden, with entertainment which included a netball match and a brass band. Over 400 people attended and it was deemed a 'roaring success'.

Annual summer camping trips to Filey had been another feature of life at the Cocoa Works prior to the war. In late July each year, 'Cocoa Boys' would gather at York station early in the morning and climb aboard a train for the coast. Again, this was an exclusively male excursion, as camping was not considered suitable for girls. Naturally, these trips were suspended for the duration of the war as many of those lads attracted by a few nights under canvas had joined the military and the coast was no longer a safe place to set up camp.

In the summer of 1915, however, four girls from the Number 1 Cream Packing Department decided that, in honour of the serving 'Cocoa Boys', they would take up the challenge of spending their summer under canvas. Misses G. Lawn, B. Haigh, L. Pink and M. Jennings pitched two tents in a field near Poppleton and established a camp which they hoped to inhabit until Christmas. The *CWM* reported this novelty with evident pride for the typically British fortitude with which these young ladies were willing to endure the hardships of life under canvas.

Their adventure was not without its pitfalls however and one of the first hazards they encountered were the cows, which insisted on barging into their tents. Not to be beaten, the girls erected a barbed wire perimeter fence around their tents and equipment. Another big headache were the wasps that swarmed around the camp; they reported killing eighteen wasps before eating breakfast one morning. When a wasp landed on a jam sandwich, one of the girls went after it with a mallet, hitting it so hard that the flattened sandwich had to be peeled off the mallet head. They took to wearing cotton wool in their ears while they slept, to prevent the many earwigs from crawling in. The girls continued to work throughout their encampment; rising at 5.30am every morning, two of the girls cycled to the Cocoa Works each day and the other two walked, if they were unable to cadge a lift on the milk cart. It is not recorded whether the girls did indeed last until Christmas.

Because the Rowntree family were so well connected in both business and politics, their employees received some distinguished visitors to the Cocoa Works. In December of 1914, Lieutenant General Sir Robert Baden-Powell paid a morale boosting visit to the works. A famous and enormously influential figure at the time, his visit had a huge impact, particularly on the young 'Cocoa Boys', whom he addressed with the following message:

> *You who read this are hoping to have a happy Christmas I expect. You probably look forward to somebody giving you a present or a treat of some kind. Supposing they don't do it? Where will you be? Your Christmas won't be so "merry and bright" as you had thought it would be. Well, I can give you a tip for guarding against this: instead of waiting for somebody to do you a good turn, do the good turn yourself, to somebody. Lend a helping hand to somebody needing it; do some little act of kindness or politeness – if it is only to smile at them; it need not cost you much but you will find that it repays you. You will feel all the happier for having done it.*

Baden-Powell had had an illustrious military career before founding the Scouting movement in 1908; he epitomised the values of teamwork, of helping one's fellow man and putting duty before individual needs. Undoubtedly, speeches like the one above would have inspired many young men to enlist for King and country, while also encouraging those on the Home Front to pull together and support one another.

Rowntree's 'Cocoa Boys' at the training camp in Harrogate – © Nestlé UK & Ireland Archive.

Letters From The Trenches

Another regular feature of the *CWM* throughout the war was the publication of letters from the men who were away fighting. The letters helped to maintain the precious sense of community that bound Rowntree's employees together. The published letters were important to those at home, because they gave an insight into what serving colleagues were experiencing, and also to the men who wrote them, who wanted to feel that they were being remembered and still had a place at the 'old Firm'. The content of the letters varied from purely factual recounting of events to descriptive, sometimes even romantic, accounts of life in the army.

34 Brawny lads from the Cocoa Works – © Nestlé UK & Ireland Archive.

Graythorne Kettlewell wrote from the training camp at Harrogate in the spring of 1915, giving details of the gruelling regime that was moulding him into shape, ready for army life proper. His day started at 6.30am with Reveille, followed by running drill from 7.15am to 7.45am. Parade started at 9.10am and finished for lunch at 12.15pm before starting for another two hours at 2.10pm. In between learning how to dig trenches, set up wire entanglements and fire a rifle at a target 25 yards distant, the men also found time for eight to ten mile route marches. This regime must have come as a shock to the system of even the fittest young men, but Kettlewell seemed to thoroughly enjoy every minute of it, taking great pride in his prowess with a rifle.

Extracts from letters published in the _CWM_

Corporal H. Noble (Offices)
At present we are in one of the hottest parts of the line, and I had a taste of shell-gas during the past week. I was at a gas demonstration yesterday, and had a taste of all the different kinds of gas used by the Germans. There is nothing to fear in any of it now, as every man is provided with a helmet which is a sure protection.

A. Sellers (Cream)
We are quite near the firing line and can hear the distant rumbling of the guns. Last night, as we marched up here, we could see quite plainly the light from the "star shells." These shells are sent up as a rocket, and when in the air they burst and illuminate the country for miles round. The Germans have been through the neighbouring village and the inhabitants have told us some sorrowful tales. One poor woman made us understand that her husband had been taken out and shot, and that she had managed to escape by hiding in a water barrel.

Driver A.P. Brown (Box Mill)
I wish to thank the Directors for the box of chocolate I received from them. There are one or two chaps from the old Firm with me, and I can tell you that these gifts are greatly appreciated.

W. Pinder (Gum)
We have been having it pretty rough and were in a big bombardment last Sunday. I had a narrow escape when a shell which failed to explode buried itself underneath me and lifted me into the air. Luckily I received no hurt. Next day a shrapnel shell burst dangerously near to me, but I am still in the best of health.

J. Appleton (Cream)
We came back on Thursday night, and four men and myself had a narrow escape. We were coming down the road to the trenches, about 1. 5 miles from the firing line and a shell burst behind us. The shock of the explosion knocked four of us down and the fifth man ran into an inn and knocked a man over who was standing with a basin of coffee in his hand. Net casualties – one basin of coffee.

J. Pickering (Cream)
We are at present lying just behind the lines after being in trenches. The houses and churches in every village we have passed through are in ruins, and it makes one long to get at grips with the Huns when one sees the poor little children and the old people whose homes have been wrecked by them.

Sapper A.J. Blows (Advertising Inspector)
We shall be glad when it is all over and we can once more live as Christians and not like savages waiting and looking for chance to rend one another to pieces.

A.S. Pattie (Almond Paste)
We are in the trenches with the W Yorks and I have seen a lot of chaps who worked at Rowntree's. It's a strange place to meet!

J. Robinson (Cream)
The Germans are only sixty yards away from us, and when they are so close they use bombs, rifle grenades and trench mortars, and the trenches are not healthy then. However, we do not have such a bad time, and the troops can always be merry.

W. Diggle (Building)
On Sunday morning I was doing my best to decrease the numbers of the German Army (and I wasn't doing badly either) when I got a bullet right through my nose, just grazing my right cheek. It is not very serious, as no bones are broken, so I expect to be going back soon when I hope to square accounts.

W.H. Mounsey (Cake)
The bullet struck me on the right cheek and was taken out of the back of my neck near the spine. My jaw was fractured and I have had two operations but now I am getting on splendidly.

Private J. Tracey (Melangeur)
I heard a noise like Krupp with a lot of R's in it and a terribly big P; then a sensation of being hit in the back by an express train and immediately sent to join the Flying Corps. When I came to I was lying in a communications trench feeling and looking as though I had come out of a conch full of 20R. My back was injured and I have lost the use of my legs for the time being.

M. Dolan (Gum)
We were due to be relieved on August 9th, but an hour before leaving the trenches the Germans began a bombardment of gas and shrapnel shells. One of the latter burst about 20 yards off and blew me several feet into the air, fracturing the left arm.

A. Catling (Fruit and Almond)
I was hit in both legs and the buttocks on June 11th. We went over the top on the 7th at Hill 60 and I managed to miss old Fritz's fire until the 11th when I was bowled over with shrapnel.

J.W. Delaney (Offices)
I had a narrow shave today. I was on a lorry to draw rations when a shell exploded six or seven yards away, killing 5 men, wounding the driver badly, next to whom I was sitting, and piercing the motor in several place. I never received a scratch. Some luck!
* . . . The train went so fast that we used to take turns at getting out and walking alongside. One fellow I believe got out and*

walked on before the train for about a mile, and then sat down
on the railside for about half an hour while the train came up;
anyway we landed her alright, but if ever I hear anyone praising
the French railways I think I'll smother them. . .

The stoicism with which the men bear their wounds is remarkable. W. H. Mounsey reports he is 'getting along splendidly' after a bullet through his cheek and W. Diggle refers to a bullet through the nose as 'not very serious'. There are one or two reports of men in hospital with shell shock, but very few discuss the horrors of war. It would be interesting to know whether those sort of letters were simply not written to the *CWM* or whether an editorial decision was made to exclude them, in case they affected morale.

Perhaps the most remarkable letter of all was written by Sergeant T. J. Williams of the 5th King's Own (Royal Lancaster) Regiment in May of 1915, though it is not clear whether he was a Rowntree's employee. Sergeant Williams had received a tin of Elect Cocoa from home in April and had stowed it safely in his pack. During the Second Battle of Ypres, at St Julien, that same month, Sergeant Williams was advancing across an open field under heavy fire, occasionally dropping to the ground to avoid shrapnel. As he dropped for the umpteenth time,

Tin of Rowntree's Cocoa Elect which saved the life of Sergeant T.J. Williams of the 5th K.O. Royal Lancaster Regiment – © Nestlé UK & Ireland Archive.

he felt something hit him hard in the back, and the force of it knocked him flat. One of his pals came scrabbling over, realising that he had been hit. Inexplicably, he could feel no pain and they could see no blood, so Sergeant Williams got to his feet and continued forward.

It was not until the following day that he had the opportunity to remove his pack and find out what had happened. As he unpacked the contents, he discovered that the Rowntree's Elect Cocoa tin had a large hole torn into one side, but not the other. The bullet had stopped inside the tin; Rowntree's Cocoa had saved Sergeant Williams' life.

For more than a century, the Cocoa Works and the Rowntree family dominated life in York. The Rowntree family employed thousands of York residents, provided facilities for the community, improved the standard of living for the poorest, built good quality, affordable housing and much more besides. During the First World War, when the whole country was in crisis, Rowntree's ensured their staff at home and overseas were supported and valued; they engaged with the war effort (despite the pro-German accusations frequently hurled at them by some) and often put people before profits.

Working for Rowntree's in York was much more than just a job, it was considered a privilege; the family's philanthropy and genuine concern for those employed by them, was never more evident than during wartime.

CHAPTER 5

1,559 Days of World War

The final year of the war was arguably the most difficult, both overseas and on the Home Front. The latter half of 1917 saw the Passchendaele offensive which lasted for some three and a half months and saw the loss of around 250,000 Allied troops. In December 1917, an armistice between Russia and the Central Powers enabled Germany to move much of her army from the Eastern Front to reinforce positions on the Western Front. The Germans took full advantage of this in March 1918, by launching an offensive so ferocious that Allied lines were pushed back further than at any time in the previous two years.

Munitions factories worked flat out to keep up with the demand for shells, with stocks becoming so depleted that the possibility of another shell crisis loomed. The situation was dire enough for the British Government to increase the upper age limit for conscription to fifty-one and for the Cabinet to make war plans as far ahead as 1920. By the end of April, however, the German offensive was all but over. Gaining so much ground had resulted in huge loss of life and the German Army simply did not have the manpower to hold and defend their positions.

Life on the British Home Front during that final year of war had changed beyond recognition from its early days. Although the country had adjusted to the demands of war, had grown used to black out restrictions and constraints on personal freedom; had learned to be suspicious of strangers, be prepared for Zeppelin raids and grown accustomed to hearing bad news; the pressures of 1917 and 1918 made life yet more difficult. Germany attempted to put Great Britain under siege; U-boats sank around one in four merchant ships carrying food and supplies into Britain, in an attempt to starve her people and break their will. In 1917 alone, 1,197 merchant ships were sunk, equating to the loss of 6,408 lives and a staggering 3,729,785 tons of cargo; by the end of April, it was estimated that Britain had only enough wheat to make six weeks' worth of bread. The rail network began to struggle through lack of coal and manpower; services often ran late and were frequently cancelled, hampering not only the movement of people but also the transport of much needed supplies.

In addition to the everyday privations of war, Britons were also subjected to the new terror of Germany's deadly Gotha and 'Giant' bombers, which were beginning to supersede the infamous Zeppelins. These heavy, long range aircraft bombed London and the South East and, rather than sneaking in under cloak of darkness as Zeppelins had done, they had the audacity to arrive in broad daylight. Faster and more manoeuvrable than Zeppelins, a Gotha bombing raid could easily take the lives of a hundred or more civilians, instead of the half-dozen or so deaths caused by a Zeppelin raid. Thus, life in Britain during the final year of war was increasingly fraught with new dangers as the enemy, no longer content with attacking purely military targets, had its sights set on the very fabric of British life.

Rationing

The inevitable consequence of Germany's U-boat campaign was a desperate shortage of food, or at least the constituents of food, such as wheat and sugar, with bread being one of the biggest problems. Bread was such a fundamental part of everyone's diet; it was taken for granted, eaten thoughtlessly and often wasted. Although bread was never officially rationed, the government embarked on a propaganda campaign to educate people into limiting their consumption and to curb profligate habits, with slogans such as: 'THE WOMAN WHO WASTES A CRUST WASTES A CARTRIDGE.'

The campaign was backed up with sanctions and fines for those who continued to be wasteful; using discarded crusts to feed his livestock could earn a farmer a fine of £50 and feeding bread to his cattle when short of cattle-cake could result in a three-month prison sentence.

As is often the way when a commodity is in short supply, the prices increase and the wealthiest are able to buy more, leaving the poorest to struggle by. After evidence emerged of malnutrition in the bottom strata of society, the Minister of Food Control, Lord Rhondda, warned that compulsory rationing was 'a grave possibility'. Towards the end of 1917, local governments had begun recommending consumption limits for their area. *The Yorkshire Herald* printed the recommended limits for the residents of York and surrounding area in November:

Bread
Man on heavy or agricultural work – 8lbs per week
Man on ordinary manual work – 7lbs per week
Man on sedentary work – 4lb 8 oz

Woman on heavy or agricultural work – 5lbs per week
Woman on ordinary manual work – 4lbs per week
Woman on sedentary work – 3lb 8 oz per week

The allowance of cereals, other than bread, is 12 oz per week
Meat 2lbs
Butter, margarine and fat 10 oz
Sugar 8 oz

Less Milk and Cheese to be used – should only be consumed by those for whom they are necessary.

In January 1918, a national rationing scheme was introduced for sugar, which allowed 8oz per person per week. In April, meat and bacon (16 oz per person), along with butter, lard and margarine (4 oz of each), were added to the ration. Other food items were rationed on a regional level and on a weekly basis depending on local conditions, with the current ration being printed in the local press. A typical local ration for York looked something like this from March 1918:

Tea: 1½ oz per head per week
Cheese: 1 oz per head per week
Bacon: No ration
Butter or margarine: 4 oz per head per week. Any farmers with a surplus supply of butter are advised to sell to their nearest shop.

A Food Control Committee was established in York to monitor and, if necessary, adjust food prices to prevent overcharging while supply was short and demand great. In March 1918, the prices for beef, mutton and offal were fixed in York and shopkeepers were ordered to prominently display price lists in their shops, to ensure that everyone was charged the same.

One local farmer wrote to the *Herald* to complain about what he felt was the unfairness of meat rationing. It had long been his custom to deliver his livestock to the cattle market in York and then purchase his own meat, at favourable rates from his butcher. Obtaining a decent cut of meat from the butcher, however, had become increasingly difficult, until finally the only meat available to him consisted of a couple of pork chops. The farmer felt this hardship keenly, arguing that his livelihood involved producing livestock which became meat to feed others, yet he was reduced to a couple of parsimonious pork chops for his Sunday lunch.

The farmer was probably not alone in feeling this way, but there was not enough meat to satisfy demand and the whole point of rationing was that everyone was treated fairly. Customers were not free to 'shop around' for rationed items, they could only buy from a shop at which they had registered and, consequently, queues would begin to form outside York's butcher's shops from 5am to ensure first pick of what meagre stock there was. To begin with, housewives could eke out the limited supply of beef by using mutton instead but, by early 1918, even mutton had become scarce and pork soon followed suit. York's butchers did what they could to satisfy their regular customers on a 'first come, first served' basis, but many of them were out of stock and closed up by noon. The police were often on hand to maintain order as the morning wore on and queues grew restless, as customers realised that the stock of meat was running low.

York's market traders faced similar problems when shoppers rushed to buy provisions at the start of the day, before the stalls were properly set up and again the police were around to ensure that disorderly scrambles did not deteriorate into violence. Rabbits and butter were among the most popular items: butter because there was often excess stock from local farms, and rabbits because they were not on ration and, at the controlled price of 1s 9d for an un-skinned rabbit or 2s for a skinned one, were affordable to all. Hares and fowls were also off ration, but were less common and therefore expensive; a hare was priced at 7s – 8s and chickens at 6s – 9s each, beyond the reach of most working households. The theft of chickens was commonplace and court appearances of those trying to sell stolen birds were a regular occurrence.

There was one instance of a man transporting some baskets of apples from the railway station to sell at York market. The baskets were covered to protect them in transit and, because the owner of the apples had not accompanied the man to market, he was not at liberty to either display or sell the apples. An expectant crowd began to gather round the man and his baskets and, despite his assurances to the contrary, they were convinced he was hiding rabbits, or maybe a stock of butter. When he repeatedly refused to uncover the stock, explaining that they were not his property, the crowd grew increasingly restless and unwilling to move on, in case they missed out. Eventually, the man and his baskets were escorted to the police station for his own safety, with a line of hopeful women and children trailing behind.

Despite all the rules, regulations and sanctions, plenty either skirted or downright flouted the official rationing rules and often paid heavily for it. York's butchers sold beef dripping off-ration, until they were sternly warned by the Food Control Committee that it counted as a lard substitute and must be sold according to ration. A David Keighley was prosecuted for selling rabbits at higher than the controlled price; greengrocer George Holmes of Micklegate was charged with not clearly displaying the price of his potatoes, while another greengrocer, Robert West, was charged with selling his potatoes above the controlled price. Market trader Emma Kershaw was fined for selling butter at a mere half-penny over the controlled price. In March, grocer William Banks was caught out selling half a pound of margarine to a Laura Newton, who was not registered there; though, as she was the housekeeper of York police station, the whole episode smacked of entrapment.

Some went as far as defending their actions in court, like Mr and Mrs Harrison, who sold damsons in contravention of the Damson (Sales) Order, 1918. The Harrisons claimed that the fruit were actually bullaces, a type of plum therefore not subject to restriction. Expert opinion was called upon to disprove this and they were fined £1 for charging £2 17s 9d for something that should have cost 22s 6d.

Even Miss Greener, the stalwart housekeeper of The Mount School, was practised in the art of obtaining supplies to feed the girls in her care. In an illuminating entry in the *Mount Magazine,* she gives a witty perspective on the privations of rationing and limited supply. Miss Greener begins by declaring that the life of a housekeeper 'in ordinary times is rather prosaic', but during the war it was like being on the Stock Exchange, 'gambling for one's next meal'. She notes the increase in the price of caraway seed, which could be bought for 6d per lb in 1914, but by 1917 could be bought for no less than 5s per lb. She tells a tongue-in-cheek tale of the 'cheese and bacon famine', a two week period when she was unable to obtain either item and struggled to prepare a nutritious and varied diet for her girls. Finally, she secured a promise of 2lbs of cheese and ½ lb of bacon and walked home 'treading on air; just think! Enough cheese for macaroni cheese all round and bacon to give a meaty flavour to the vegetarian dishes!'

Shopping in wartime required as much tact and diplomacy as 'working in the Diplomatic Service itself', she continued, before describing the range of tactics she used to get around shopkeepers. Playing 'meek' with a shopkeeper is most 'efficacious', while being prepared to treat the advances of a flirtatious shop man as a 'huge joke' helps to 'soften his heart', but lose your temper with him and you could starve for the rest of the war. Miss Greener was registered with the pork butcher Scott's on Low Petergate and evidently had a good relationship with the proprietor. When she sent payment of the Mount School's account to Mr Scott one morning, the messenger returned with the bill unpaid, due to the 'nasty looking crowd' gathered at his shop – no doubt growing restless as the meat stock ran low. Miss Greener took to approaching the shop via a side alley and waiting in Mr Scott's kitchen while the account was settled, thereby securing a regular – and generous – supply of whatever meat was available for the school.

In truth, almost everyone was trying to get a bit more than they were entitled to, or to make some extra cash while times were hard, yet most people were thoroughly censorious towards anyone else unfortunate enough to get caught in the act.

Tank Week

Despite the increasing complications of wartime life, the patriotic spirt remained intact and one of the ways it manifested was in a continuing willingness to support the war financially. The National Savings movement had been established in 1916 and encouraged people to save or invest their money in bonds, certificates and savings stamps, which enabled the government to fund production of artillery and munitions. In September 1916, Britain introduced tanks into battle and although they had limited success to begin with, they came into their own at the Battle of Cambrai in November 1917. Although the efficacy of tanks in this battle has been debated in the intervening years, at the time tanks were hailed as the heroes.

Futuristic and unstoppable, tanks were billed as the means by which Britain would win the war. Unfortunately, they were also incredibly expensive, costing £5,000 each. The solution to this was a massive, nationwide fundraising initiative which would capture the public imagination and engender a sense of patriotic competition: six battle-scarred tanks would tour the country, spending a week each in as many large towns and cities as could accommodate them.

The whole campaign opened in London just weeks after the Battle of Cambrai; tank number 130 – 'Nelson' – was driven into Trafalgar Square as the focal point for the launch of the 'Tank Bank' War Bonds scheme. Crowds thronged to view the iron monster; the band of the Coldstream Guards played tunes to stir the soul; stars of stage and screen along with members of the aristocracy, all turned out to pledge support and buy war bonds. The Lord Mayor of York, W. A. Forster Todd, also appeared and made a patriotic speech about the importance of tanks in winning the war and how much the people of York were looking forward to hosting their very own 'tank week' in the coming months.

It was tank number 130 itself that arrived by train at Foss Island Goods Yard, York on 11 February 1918. Excitement in the city had been mounting prior to 'Nelson's' arrival, with workers and schoolchildren asking for time off so they could witness the mighty beast arrive. It took many hours of careful handling to move 'Nelson' off his rail transport, under the spellbound gaze of many spectators watching from the city walls, but by 8pm he was finally ready for his journey into York city centre the following morning.

'Nelson' left Foss Island Goods Yard at 8.30am on Tuesday, 12 February and set off along a bunting-strewn route crowded with onlookers. The tank's route took it along the Barbican Road, past the

Tank No 130, 'Nelson' during 'Tank Week' February 1918 – Courtesy of Hugh Murray.

Tank No 130, 'Nelson' with Lord Mayor during 'Tank Week' February 1918 – Courtesy of Hugh Murray.

Cattle Market, onto Paragon Street, along Fishergate, then Piccadilly, arriving at Market Place by 9am, where it was given pride of place for the rest of that week. An official opening ceremony commenced at midday, hosted by the Lord Mayor and other civic dignitaries.

The sense of competition between towns and cities was immense. The town raising the most money during their Tank Week could claim to have done more than anywhere else in support of the war effort. The Mayor stated that 'Nelson' had had a very successful week in Bradford, raising a staggering £13 13s 8d per head of the population and, to beat that, York needed to raise in excess of £1,100,000,. He added that he had every confidence in the citizens of York meeting the challenge and to start the fund off the city Corporation had donated £50,000.

The 'Tank Bank' was open from 10am to 8pm each day and a temporary Post Office was constructed in Market Place to handle the many hundreds of citizens wanting to play their part in buying a tank. Although people were encouraged to invest as much as they could afford, (some contributed hundreds of pounds), even the purchase of a £5 War Bond was welcomed. The fundraising was not limited to Market Place though – the whole city took part, with a Prize Scheme which meant that every single bond or certificate bought, no matter how small, entitled the purchaser to a place in a draw with a £100 cash prize.

After the end of the war, the National War Savings Committee presented tanks to the 265 towns and cities which had contributed so generously to their purchase. While some towns, like nearby Harrogate, declined the offer, preferring not to be reminded of the horrors of war, most accepted the gift willingly. The city of York was presented with its gift tank in July 1919 and it spent many years on display in a corner of Tower Gardens. Sadly, there was little funding available for the upkeep of these gift tanks in the post-war years and most rusted quietly away, before being scrapped in the Thirties.

Escapades and Epidemics

Life in York was not all about the war, of course. The newspapers were regularly punctuated with other stories; of thefts and murders; births, deaths and marriages; drunken rowdiness and provincial life. Every now and again, something so out of the ordinary happened that, just for a brief period of time, the war took a back seat. One such incident involved a middle-aged lady and the giddy heights of York Minster.

Miss Monnington, the middle-aged lady in question, was on parole from The Retreat, a residential home that took an enlightened approach to caring for those with mental health issues. As Miss Monnington was generally a quiet and trustworthy resident, she was allowed to go for days out in York by herself, which she had done several times without incident. On Friday, 2 November 1918, however, Miss Monnington decided that she had had enough of the quiet life.

Then, as now, the minster was open to visitors during the day but closed when a service was taking place. It is thought that Miss Monnington had visited the minster during the late afternoon and climbed the 213 steps of the Central Tower when it was accessible to the public. As the day's visitors left, Miss Monnington was overlooked and the door to the tower was locked. During evensong, she presented herself to the city from the highest parapet of the Central Tower. The parapet itself was no more than 10 inches wide and some 221 feet above the ground, but Miss Monnington appeared to have no fear. Kicking off her shoes and letting them drop to the pavement far below, quickly followed by her stockings, Miss Monnington began performing what the horrified crowd gathered beneath described as a 'wild dance'. When she had finished this incredible feat, she simply sat down with her bare legs dangling over the parapet, taking in the view, appearing quite unaware of the sheer panic she was causing down below.

The Clerk of Works, Mr R. C. Green, was fetched and a rescue plan was formulated. A group of servicemen from the crowd volunteered to help distract Miss Monnington, while Mr Green attempted to rescue her. The servicemen climbed the tower steps and engaged the lady in conversation. She appeared quite calm and happily chatted to the men while Mr Green rested a ladder from the top of the tower against the parapet wall and quietly climbed up behind her. Once there, he grabbed her from behind and pulled her back down with him to safety. The shock of this infuriated Miss Monnington and she fought wildly against being taken back down the 213 steps. Incredibly, no one was injured during Miss Monnington's escapade, which provided the residents of York with the most improbable diversion from talk of war, rationing and influenza.

The influenza pandemic that swept the globe during 1918 and 1919 killed as many as 40 million people worldwide, three times more than were killed in the whole of the war. The first major outbreak of influenza in Britain was reported in Glasgow in May 1918 and by June the virus had reached London; some 228,000 people were to die of influenza in Britain over the ensuing months.

Influenza featured heavily in both the *Yorkshire Press* and *The Herald* in the latter half of 1918, where reports of illness and death sat alongside optimistic adverts for influenza medicines, pills and cures. At the end of October 1918, the *Herald* reported 'No Sign Of Abatement' in the epidemic and gave details of the 'Heavy Death Toll In York'. During the last week of October, there had been twenty-eight deaths from influenza in the city and a further eleven from pneumonia, making a total of forty deaths from influenza and twenty-one from pneumonia in the previous three weeks alone. At the beginning of November, only three schools in the city were still open as usual, the rest were closed due to the epidemic.

The Health Committee discussed the possibility of closing all places of amusement in the city, but decided that this was a step too far for the sake of the businesses concerned and for general morale. Instead they introduced a series of stringent measures to try to alleviate the risk of spreading the illness in public places: children under the age of fourteen (being more vulnerable to contagion) were to be excluded from all houses of entertainment, except the Theatre Royal; the various cinemas in the city were asked to allow at least one hour to elapse between the afternoon and evening performances and the Empire and Opera House theatre, three quarters of an hour. This was to allow adequate ventilation of the auditorium between one audience and the next. The management of the Theatre Royal was asked to provide a free flush of air throughout the auditorium for half an hour before and after each performance and for a quarter of an hour or more in the interval.

It was through compromises like this that the people of York continued to live as normal a life as possible in increasingly difficult and demanding circumstances. Yet, now, as if losing loved ones to battle was not enough to worry about, there was an ever-increasing likelihood that your family could be snatched from under your very nose in your own home. When Mrs Lydia Brown of Hungate died of influenza in October, her two daughters, aged eleven and sixteen, followed suit the next week and there was another report from Hungate of seven members of the same household all being seriously ill. The increasing death rate in the city caused major problems for York

Cemetery; there were simply not enough staff to cope with the number of burials and they applied to the military for men to help with the grave digging. During the last nine days of October, there were 110 burials at the cemetery, against the seasonal average of thirty.

Armistice

Just when life was seeming bleaker than ever, the war ended. It was what everyone had longed and prayed for, yet dared not hope for. The armistice was signed at 5am on 11 November 1918 and signalled the end of hostilities from 11am that same day. Despite the agreement being made, fighting continued right up until the 11am deadline, with many men at the front entirely unaware of it until the shooting actually stopped.

At 10.55am in London, Lloyd George emerged from 10 Downing Street to read a short statement:

> *At eleven o'clock this war will be over. We have won a great victory and we are entitled to a bit of shouting.*

Five minutes later, at precisely 11am, Big Ben chimed for the first time since August 1914.

In York, the Union Jack was raised above the Mansion House during the morning, signalling to the citizens that something was afoot. Crowds began to gather outside and rumours abounded when, at precisely 11am, the Mayor stepped out to announce news of the armistice. York erupted into a frenzy of celebration; just as Big Ben had burst into life in London, so the bells of York Minster pealed for the first time in over four years. The Mayor went on to say that the terms of the armistice were as yet unknown, but he trusted that 'they would be of such a stringent character as would prevent the Germans ever renewing the terrible tragedy which we had just brought to a successful conclusion.'

Within the hour, a special edition of *The Yorkshire Evening Press* was on sale, with the heading:

THE MIGHTY DRAMA OF 1,559 DAYS OF WORLD-WAR
Newsboys struggled to fight their way through the crowds on Coney Street, in order to take the news to other parts of the city and the Mayor requested that all businesses close for the remainder of the day and

allow their workers a holiday to celebrate the great news. Rowntree's responded by allowing their workforce to finish immediately, though they still received full pay for the day. The North Eastern Railway Co's Carriage and Wagon Works and the Co-operative Society's places of business also closed for the day.

The initial widespread joy at news of the armistice was tinged with feelings of sadness and sorrow. For some, it was a confusing time as they laughed and cried alongside those rejoicing, while remembering loved ones who would never come home again.

Soon after the bells had begun their victory peal, citizens made their way to the minster in accordance with Dean's request for a service of thanksgiving. At 12.30pm, there was a service the like of which had not been witnessed within living memory. Well over 10,000 people crowded into the historic nave, transept and choir to join in giving thanks for the end of war. No one was dressed in their Sunday best, because this was no formal gathering. Instead, it was a spontaneous, disordered, motley crowd of citizens: shopkeepers, housewives, workers in white aprons, ragged little urchins from the streets, all fresh from their daily routines.

It did not take long for the citizens to put out flags and bunting.

Millfield Road, York Peace Celebrations, November 1918 – Courtesy of Hugh Murray.

Coney Street became a blaze of colour first, quickly followed by Micklegate, Blossom Street, Holgate, Rougier Street, Walmgate, Hungate and Layerthorpe – all rivalling the streets in the centre of the city. Flags were hung out from almost every window of both mansions and tenements. People bedecked themselves with patriotic colours, and the drapers' shops were busier than they had been for many a day.

Throughout the afternoon, the main streets of the city were filled with crowds of people wearing red, white and blue ribbons and singing lustily. By this time all the shops were closed and the buildings could scarcely be seen for bunting. One gallant and perhaps inebriated soldier was so overjoyed on hearing the news, that he 'fell upon the neck of a passing postman and kissed him passionately'. Aeroplanes flew over the city performing loop-the-loops to the delight of spectators.

Soldiers too were given a half-day holiday and one party paraded the streets headed by a kettle drummer, while at the Fulford Road Barracks hundreds of men flocked to the parade ground, where singing and dancing broke out. One brave lad clambered up the barracks clock tower with an enormous Union Jack in tow, which he struggled for half an hour to hoist, amidst encouraging cheers from his comrades.

The lively scenes continued into the early hours of the morning, as thousands paraded streets illuminated by displays of fireworks and light flooding from houses now free to leave blinds undrawn at last.

Remembrance and the Future

What was there to do now?Four long, hard, devastating years of war were over. There was barely a town or village in the country which had not lost members of their community. A generation of young men had been decimated and many of those who had returned were irrevocably changed. The fighting may have ended but for those who had returned, physically and mentally scarred, the legacy of war would live on for many years to come.

It was vitally important to concentrate on the future, to begin the business of rebuilding lives, both figuratively and literally. In many cities, the slum clearance programmes, which had been halted because of the war began again in earnest. After surviving four years of war, families deserved better homes and none more so than returning servicemen. Prior to the outbreak of war in York, an average of eighty houses a year were being built as part of the city's slum clearance plans, with a further 220 houses scheduled on the Tang Hall estate, but in the years 1915-18 only fifty-four houses were built.

In 1919, York City Council estimated that around 300 houses were needed to meet the shortage, in addition to the 950 now needed to rehouse those displaced by slum clearance. This house-building programme fitted in with a national 'Homes fit for Heroes' policy, launched in 1919, which set about building 'cottage estates' throughout the 1920s; these estates would consist of houses built in groups of four or six, set among gardens, trees and privet hedges. Build quality was of the utmost importance, because these homes were designed to improve the standard of living for working people.

It was also important for those left behind, for those who had survived, to remember the fallen. Britain had never lost so many young men in such a brutal war; there had been no need for local, as well as national remembrance. After the Great War, however, formal

Heroes of York Portraits– Courtesy of Hugh Murray.

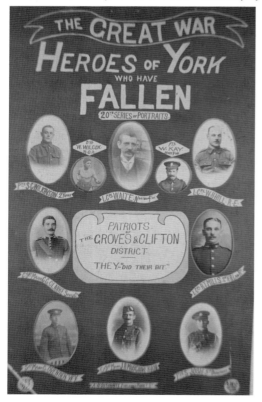 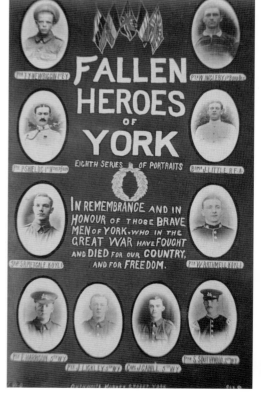

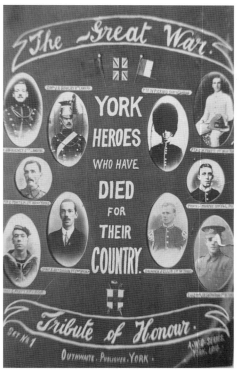
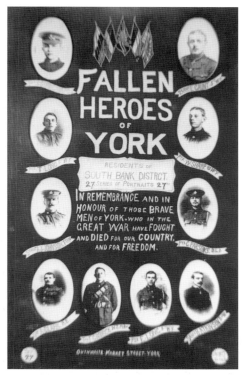

Heroes of York Portraits – Courtesy of Hugh Murray.

York Comrades Memorial – August 1919 – Courtesy of Hugh Murray.

remembrance seemed the only way to cope with, and move on from, the loss.

From 1919 onwards, war memorials were erected in every village, town and city in Britain, with the exception of forty so called 'Thankful Villages' which had been fortunate enough not to lose any member of their community to the war. In the city of York alone, some thirty war memorials were erected to commemorate York's 1,160 war dead – from the grand white obelisk of the York Citizens Memorial on Leeman Road, right down to the simple plaques adorning the walls of parish churches, not a single one of York's fallen were forgotten.

The Post Office has its own memorial to commemorate the twenty-six fallen postal workers; the York YMCA remembers twenty colleagues on a bronze plaque; even four female munition workers killed by an explosion at the munitions factory in 1916 are commemorated by a memorial plaque in York Cemetery. The

Tank awarded to York after the war, situated in Tower Gardens – Courtesy of Hugh Murray.

York Citizens Memorial, Leeman Road – © K. Burnham.

ERECTED TO THE MEMORY
OF THOSE MEMBERS OF THE YORK
AND DISTRICT POST OFFICE STAFF
WHO FELL IN THE GREAT WAR 1914–1919 ·

H·BENSON	A·HORNER	J·W·J·OUTHWAITE
A·L·B·BLUNT	H·HORNER	F·POULTER
P·BUCKLE	G·JACKSON	T·PRITCHARD
C·CLARK	S·H·LEEDER	F·R·RAINE
L·A·DOUTHWAITE	W·H·MACAULAY	A·G·SADLER
C·FAIRBURN	W·MARSHALL	G·SHEARMAN
G·FOTHERGILL	A·MORRILL	J·TISSIMAN
G·E·FOX	F·MORRIS	A·UPTON
W·GORDON		E·WINTERBURN

PASS FRIEND   ALL'S WELL

York Post Office Memorial plaque – © K. Burnham.

headquarters of the North Eastern Railway were situated in York, so it was natural that a memorial should be constructed in the city to commemorate the 2,236 men employed by the N. E. R who had lost their lives. This imposing monument, designed by Edwin Lutyens, was built in 1923 and still occupies a commanding position on Station Rise.

Rowntree & Co held a memorial service on Sunday, 12 September 1919 to commemorate its fallen employees, at which a specially commissioned plaque was unveiled. The speeches delivered during this service are still extremely moving as their fellow workers were remembered:

> *your loss is our loss; the grief in your little family is shared by the big family at the Cocoa Works, where those who have fallen spent so much of their lives. We miss them in the workrooms; they are ever in our thoughts. Their voices are fresh in my ears and the ghosts of the past stay yet in the classrooms, the playing field, the camp, and the Works.*
>
> *The hideousness of their circumstances was only endurable through the ideals which called them from the factory to the Front. The vision which they saw, perhaps in a crude way, was*

a world in which there should be no more war, no more oppression of little nations, no more tyranny of military autocrats and crushing burden of armaments. Their dream has faded into the light of common day. It has been cynically said that we won the War and lost the Peace.

When Seebohm Rowntree rose to unveil the Memorial Tablet, he did so with these words:

Our debt to the fallen cannot be redeemed merely by a tablet. It was not hatred of the enemy, but their ideals for England and the future of mankind and their profound belief that Right was greater than Might that inspired the men who went to the War.

As the tablet was finally unveiled, the Last Post was sounded by four trumpeters of the 7th (Queen's Own) Hussars.

No doubt the content of this particular memorial service was echoed in every other service that took place in York over the years immediately following the war. The many memorials provide a perpetual reminder of 'the war to end all wars' and the loss of life in each parish and community. York City Council felt that all these separate memorials with their lists of names were an insufficient tribute to the brave and the gallant. They wanted a single memorial which would forever record each and every York man, and woman, who had given their life; what they conceived was *The King's Own Book of York Heroes*.

Designed by the artist Edwin Ridsdale Tate, *The King's Own Book of York Heroes* is approximately 2 feet long and 9 inches thick, weighing 9st 4lb, it is one of the largest books in the world. It was lovingly created by local craftsmen; the cover is made of English oak, courtesy of the Superintendent of Works at the North Eastern Railway Company's carriage and wagon department, carved by a Mr George Hudson. The book contains not only the names of the fallen, but also obituaries and photographs, which were collected and collated by Mr Adams of the *The Yorkshire Evening Press*. Although almost all the names belong to men, two women are also included: Eveline Hodgson, a military nurse who died in Salonika, Greece; and Betty Stevenson, who worked for the YMCA in France. The book was completed and presented to the minster in time for the second anniversary of the Armistice; four months later, it was taken to Buckingham Palace to be signed by King George V. Several pages were left blank at the back of the book, because the city council knew that they might have to continue adding names as the years went by. Names of the fallen are still being added to this day – seven in the last year alone – as the descendants of soldiers come forward.

The city of York has a long and chequered history; its character has been shaped through the centuries by invasion, occupation, industrial revolution and economic growth. The four years of the Great War seem but a blip in this extensive history and yet no other event before it took the lives of so many of its citizens in so short a space of time. No other event had engendered such patriotism, nor caused such suspicion and mistrust among its residents.

The Great War left an indelible mark on the city and its people, the effects of which, thanks to the many acts of commemoration, will be remembered for generations to come.

Sources

The newspaper archives of the *Yorkshire Evening Press* and *Herald*

York Explore Library
Library Square
York
Y01 7DS
www.york.gov.uk

The Cocoa Works Magazine 1914 – 1918 Nestlé UK & Ireland Archive

Accessed at:
The Borthwick Institute for Archives
University of York
Heslington
York
YO10 5DD
www.york.ac.uk/borthwick

The British Library

Boston Spa
Wetherby
West Yorkshire
LS23 7BQ
www.bl.uk

Institute for Public Understanding of the Past (IPUP)

Humanities Research Centre
Berrick Saul Building

University of York
York
YO10 5DD
www.york.ac.uk/ipup/

York Castle Museum

Eye of York
York
YO1 9RY
www.yorkcastlemuseum.org.uk/page/index.aspx

The Liddle Collection

The Brotherton Library
University of Leeds
Leeds
LS2 9JT
http://library.leeds.ac.uk/special-collections-liddle-collection

www.yorkandthegreatwar.com – York's WW1 Roll of Honour and details of war memorials.

Select Bibliography

Adie, Kate. *Fighting On The Home Front, The Legacy of Women in World War One*, London: Hodder & Stoughton, 2013

Arthur, Max. *Forgotten Voices Of The Great War*, London: Random House, 2002

Bilton, David. *The Home Front in The Great War, Aspects of the conflict 1914-1918*, Barnsley: Pen & Sword Books Ltd, 2003

Catchpool, Corder. *On Two Fronts*, London: George Allen & Unwin Ltd, 1919

De-Groot, Gerald J. *Blighty: British Society in the Era of the Great War*, Harlow: Addison Wesley Longman Ltd,1996

Newman, V. *We Also Served: The Forgotten Women of The First World War*, Barnsley: Pen & Sword Books Ltd, 2014

Paxman, Jeremy. *Great Britain's Great War*, London: Penguin Books, 2013

Peacock, A.J. *York In The Great War 1914 – 1918,* York: The York Settlement Trust, 1993.

Rubenstein, David. *York Friends and the Great War*: Borthwick Paper No 96, Borthwick Institute of Historical Research, 1999.

Shiels, Sarah. *Among Friends, The Story of The Mount School:* London: James & James (Publishers) Ltd, 2007

Taylor, A.J.P. *How Wars Begin*, London: Hamish Hamilton Ltd, 1979

Index

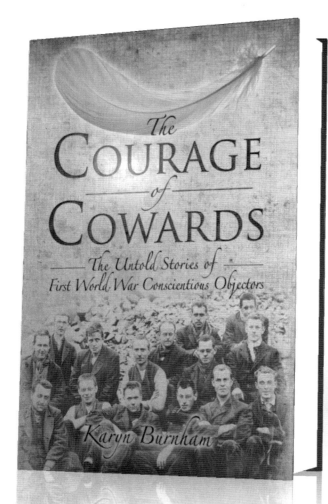

9781781592953 •
144 pages • HB •
16pp B&W plates • £16.99

The Courage of Cowards is a fascinating insight into the First World War through the eyes of the men who felt compelled not to fight. From memoirs, letters and official records, Karyn Burnham reveals the untold stories of conscientious objectors who had the courage to stand by their beliefs when the country was against them.

Pilloried, bullied, imprisoned and even threatened with death, these ordinary men had remarkable experiences: serving in the Non-Combatant Corps; dealing with the carnage of the Western Front with the Friends Ambulance Unit or defying authority and playing no part whatsoever in the war.

Discover the true stories of men like Charles Dingle, a medical orderly, who helped evacuate wounded soldiers under heavy bombardment on the Western Front; like Jack Foister, secretly shipped to France and sentenced to death for his beliefs.

In January 1916, with the death toll mounting and the number of volunteers no longer meeting the voracious demands of the war, Prime Minister Asquith took the radical step of introducing conscription. For the first time in British history, the Government had the right to call the ordinary working man to arms. Those who opposed war for religious or political reasons were about to face the biggest battle of their lives.

WHAT THE CRITICS SAID:

'Told in an accessible and immediate style without sentimentalising the facts.'   THE BOOKSELLER

Order your copy now by calling **01226 734222**
or order online via our website: **www.pen-and-sword.co.uk**